A Principled Constitution?

A Principled Constitution?

Four Skeptical Views

Steven D. Smith
Larry Alexander
James Allan
and Maimon Schwarzschild

LEXINGTON BOOKS
Lanham • Boulder • New York • London

Published by Lexington Books
An imprint of The Rowman & Littlefield Publishing Group, Inc.
4501 Forbes Boulevard, Suite 200, Lanham, Maryland 20706
www.rowman.com

86-90 Paul Street, London EC2A 4NE

Copyright © 2022 by The Rowman & Littlefield Publishing Group, Inc.

All rights reserved. No part of this book may be reproduced in any form or by any electronic or mechanical means, including information storage and retrieval systems, without written permission from the publisher, except by a reviewer who may quote passages in a review.

British Library Cataloguing in Publication Information Available

Library of Congress Cataloging-in-Publication Data Available

ISBN 978-1-66691-147-3 (cloth)
ISBN 978-1-66691-149-7 (paperback)
ISBN 978-1-66691-148-0 (electronic)

Contents

Acknowledgments   vii

PART I: A PRINCIPLED CONSTITUTION?   1
Introduction   3

Chapter One: Unpretentious Beginnings: The Merely Legal Constitution   5
Steven D. Smith

PART II: FOUR (SOMEWHAT) SKEPTICAL PERSPECTIVES   73

Chapter Two: The Not-Your-Ancestors' Principle-Plush Constitution   39
Steven D. Smith

Chapter Three: So You Think You Want a Constitution of Principles   65
Larry Alexander

Chapter Four: Mushy Constitutional Principles Enabling Puffed-Up Judicial Policymaking: I'm Against, on Principle   75
James Allan

Chapter Five: The Power—and Peril—of Principle   91
Maimon Schwarzschild

Bibliography   103

Index   109

About the Authors   113

Acknowledgments

The authors wish to express our gratitude for the important assistance we have received from Elizabeth Parker, Sasha Nuñez, and Sara Noakes.

PART I

A Principled Constitution?

Introduction

Is the United States Constitution the embodiment of certain principles? The authors of this book—and there are four of us—for a variety of reasons, and with somewhat different emphases, believe the answer is "no." Those who authored the Constitution no doubt all believed in liberty, equality, and, with caveats, republican self-government—values, or if you will, "principles." But they had different conceptions of those values or principles and what those values or principles entailed for constituting a government. So although the Constitution they fashioned reflected in some sense their principles, the Constitution itself was a specific list of do's and don'ts that its authors hoped would gain the allegiance of all the newly independent and sovereign states.

In what follows, we four authors will each give our separate accounts for why the Constitution does not and should not embody principles, at least not directly. Steven Smith, in chapter 1, recounts how the Constitution's framers were forced to compromise or even betray their basic principles on matters like representation, slavery, and the nature of the union in order to devise a proposal that might save the nation from disintegration. Then, in chapter 2, Smith critiques the views of three more contemporary proponents of a "principled Constitution"—Herbert Wechsler, Ronald Dworkin, and Jack Balkin.

In chapter 3, Larry Alexander casts doubt on the existence of distinctly *legal* principles and discusses the difficulties and implications of attempting to incorporate *moral* principles in a document that will be judicially enforced. In chapter 4, James Allan elaborates further on the problem of judicial enforcement of principles, particularly its tendency to transfer power of governance from elected legislators to judges. And in chapter 5, Maimon Schwarzschild discusses the role arguments over principles have played outside the courts in political discourse.

The reader should, therefore, not expect either a unity of thought or of style in these chapters, Rather, what the reader can expect is what our title advertises: four somewhat skeptical views about the existence and desirability of a "principled Constitution."

Chapter One

Unpretentious Beginnings
The Merely Legal Constitution

Steven D. Smith

We've heard it countless times, of course—the story of the American Founding and the creation of the Constitution. But the story still bears repeating. Especially in times of national discouragement or distress—times like ours—when wisdom and reassurance are desperately needed. Let's see; how does the story go again?

A CELEBRATORY, PROFOUNDLY MISLEADING STORY—AND ITS EQUALLY MISLEADING SPINOFFS

Well, it begins with a feisty band of patriots who, animated by noble notions like "all men are created equal" and "unalienable rights" including "life, liberty, and the pursuit of happiness," declare their independence from a suffocating foreign monarchy. For the next several years, these patriots and their ragtag, sparsely supplied, sometimes barefoot army fight a bloody, barbarous war against the world's supreme military power—and, improbably, wind up winning that war. Now, against all odds, they are free.

Alas, in their newly gained independence, Americans neglect the noble ideals that brought them together and inspired their revolution. Instead, they separate into competing states and classes and degenerate into sordid internecine squabbling over land and tariffs and paper money and accumulated debts. And the national government is so feckless and insipid that it lacks the power, or the will, or both, to guide the new nation toward the realization of its revolutionary vision.

And so the nation's more farsighted leaders gather in a constitutional convention, in Philadelphia, and boldly draft up a new document that significantly strengthens the central government and that recommits the nation to lofty principles and ideals: liberty, equality, justice, and the common good. The document expounding these commitments—the Constitution—would come to serve as an inspiration to Americans for the rest of the Republic's existence. And not only to Americans: an eminent nineteenth-century British statesman, William Gladstone, observed that "the American Constitution is, so far as I can see, the most wonderful work ever struck off at a given time by the brain and purpose of man."

Humans are imperfect, of course, and the ideals embraced by the Constitution are sufficiently ambitious that they cannot be fully realized all at once. So in addition to being inspirational, the new Constitution would also be aspirational. Despite (or because of) that aspirational quality, it has stood as a guide and beacon to Americans ever since, as they—as *we*, We the People—have striven to realize its majestic vision.

The story is an ennobling one—one that Americans can celebrate, and recall with pride. It is also, as we will see in the next chapter, a story perfectly crafted—indeed, suspiciously well suited—to support the commitments and aspirations of modern constitutionalists of a progressive bent.

To be sure, the celebratory story also has its inconvenient features. One inconvenience, albeit one that does not seem to trouble current constitutionalists much, is that just on the level of mundane historical fact, the story is, well . . . not actually true.

Some of it is true. Quite a lot of it. The first part, about declaring independence and invoking "unalienable rights," and about fighting a difficult war, is largely true, if simplified and selective (as stories necessarily are). And once the war was won, Americans *did* descend into bickering over trade and land and debts. As a result, a distinguished group of concerned political leaders *did* meet in Philadelphia and draft up a new Constitution, which *did* allocate significantly expanded powers to the restructured national government.

All of this is true. And yet the celebratory story is profoundly deceptive in two crucial respects.

Its first error is a subtle one. To say (as we routinely do) that the framers—the Philadelphia delegates and their political allies—had the purpose of strengthening the powers of the national government is in one sense entirely accurate and in another sense deeply misleading. It is as if an emergency paramedic, asked why he had applied a tourniquet to a person who was bleeding out, were to explain, "I did it because I thought it would improve his health." Strictly speaking, it is surely true that a living person is healthier than one who has bled to death. And yet this is the sort of thing a doctor would say in prescribing a new exercise regimen or a medication to remedy high blood pressure. With respect to applying the tourniquet, by contrast, the proper explanation would say: "I did it because otherwise *he was going to die!*"

In a similar way, the statesmen-politicians who wrote and supported and adopted the Constitution acted on the conviction that without a new, stronger constitution, the nation was going to disintegrate. Their most fundamental aim was not to strengthen the national government with the aim of promoting a more prosperous economy or a more just political regime (although no doubt they did hope for those things too), but rather to create and maintain a nation.

In that respect, founding-era debates over national power were distinctly unlike modern debates about national power (between "conservatives" and New Deal "liberals" and contemporary "progressives," for example) that superficially resemble them. In modern times (at least until very recently), we have typically taken for granted that we are and will continue to be a nation, and that the national government will continue to exist and function.[1] The controversial questions have been about how large that government should be, how much power and responsibility it should have. So, we argue about whether a stronger or weaker national government is more conducive to prosperity or social justice or a clean environment or whatever. By contrast, the founders wanted a stronger national government because they believed that otherwise there would soon be *no nation at all*.

If we fail to understand this point, we fail also to understand why the Philadelphia delegates did the things they did—both the things we tend to admire and the things we deplore—and why the states ended up reluctantly ratifying their work product even though most Americans probably did not like or want it. And we fail as well to comprehend the essential character of the document that the framers created and called (and that we continue to call) "the Constitution."

Which brings us to the second way in which the celebratory story misrepresents our history. The Constitution drafted in Philadelphia was primarily, overwhelmingly, almost exclusively, a *legal* document. It did *not* articulate, or commit the nation to, noble ideals of liberty, equality, or human brotherhood. An opposite claim would be closer to the truth: in the interest of holding the nation together, the Constitution deliberately eschewed, compromised, or suspended the nation's commitment to fundamental ideals and principles.

To be sure, that contrary description is not quite true either; or at least it is less than the full truth. But the Constitution's relation to "principles"—principles of justice, of political morality—was complex and ambiguous. The document was emphatically *not* the affirmation of lofty ideals and principles that modern constitutionalists have so often wished that it were (and have accordingly pretended that it is).

Justice William Brennan once declared that he viewed the Constitution as "a sublime oration on the dignity of man."[2] It is a noble and edifying sentiment, no doubt, but one can only wonder: had the Justice ever actually read the document? (And in fact, as a law student at Harvard, Brennan had elected not to take the course on constitutional law.[3])

In questioning the celebratory story, however, we should not make the mistake of endorsing either of two familiar alternatives that are themselves offshoots of, and dependent on, that story. One is a darker variant that we might describe as the "hypocrisy" story. The other is a more hopeful version sometimes presented as a "redemption" story.

Both of these versions agree with the celebratory story in asserting or assuming that the Constitution contained commitments to noble ideals. But the hypocrisy story, alluring at a time when removing statues and denouncing our wicked predecessors has become almost an obsession in some quarters, goes on to reproach the framers and the document they created for compromising or sacrificing those ideals—especially although not exclusively with respect to slavery. The Constitution, in this view, committed the nation to principles of justice and equality but then proceeded to establish a government that conspired or at least acquiesced in rampant injustices—to slaves, to Native Americans, to women, to the poorer classes. The "redemption" version is similar except that it looks backward with more mercy and forward with more hopefulness, and it thus depicts the nation's history as an ongoing project of "redeeming" the lofty but imperfectly realized principles and "promises" contained in the Constitution.[4]

Both of these variants are misguided for the same reason that the more purely celebratory story is: they assume that the Constitution was a document affirming lofty principles—principles that the nation either proceeded to betray or else has been in process of "redeeming." But in fact the premise upon which depend both the charge of hypocrisy and the promise of redemption is, not to put too fine a point on it, simply false. The Constitution was not that kind of document.

To see how this is so, and to understand what sort of thing the Constitution actually was, we will need to revisit some aspects of the founding that are for the most part familiar enough but that modern tellings of the constitutional story tend to downplay, obfuscate, or interpret away.

AVERTING ANARCHY

We need to begin by describing what the Constitution's framers were trying to do—or, perhaps more precisely, what they were trying desperately to *avoid*. In the years between the end of the Revolutionary War and the Philadelphia convention, leading American figures like George Washington and Benjamin Franklin came to believe that the loosely confederated alliance of states was on the verge of breaking up. And in a recent study, historian Joseph Ellis argues that they were right.[5]

We misconceive the situation, Ellis argues, when we say that the national government was weak and in need of strengthening: in reality there was no "nation" and no real national "government" to strengthen. Upon declaring their independence from England, rather, the thirteen states became in effect thirteen separate sovereignties who entered into a loose confederation—something similar to NATO—mainly for the purpose of defending themselves against British subjugation. Once the war was won, these states had little inclination to respect or continue that confederation, much less to strengthen it.

Indeed, even while the war was still being fought and was very much in the balance, George Washington was doubtful of the possibility of national unity. In a letter written in 1780, Washington acknowledged that "I see one head gradually changing into thirteen."[6] Later, no longer under the existential threat of reconquest by England, the states drifted even more definitely into their separate trajectories.

And so Washington and other leaders met in Philadelphia because they believed that without drastic measures, the states would soon break into separate entities, or perhaps into a few separate confederacies. The goal of the Philadelphia convention was thus not to strengthen the national government but rather to create and preserve a nation—a union. Or at least the goal was to create a new and stronger national government *as a means* of creating and preserving a nation, or a union.

And why was *union*, or nationhood, such a preeminent objective? A cynic might say that Washington and Madison and company wanted a union because such an arrangement would be conducive to their economic interests and political ambitions. That observation would contain a measure of truth, at least for some of the framers (Alexander Hamilton comes quickly to mind), but it would also greatly diminish and distort their full motivations. What was most fundamentally at stake, they thought, was not just a prosperous economy but rather the fate of republican government, not just here but everywhere.

Thus, at a particularly tense moment when the Philadelphia convention was on the verge of collapse, Virginia's governor Edmund Randolph pleaded with the delegates that "the salvation of the republic was at stake," and that if the republic were not secured now there would probably never be another opportunity.[7] James Madison agreed: "it was more than probable we were now digesting a plan which in its operation would decide forever the fate of republican government."[8] Alexander Hamilton concurred.[9] We might borrow forward from Abraham Lincoln's classic speech: the delegates believed that their achievement or failure would determine whether "government of the people, by the people, for the people, [would] perish from the earth."

In this perspective, the consequences of failure, and hence of disunion, would be catastrophic. Benjamin Franklin put the matter poignantly:

> We shall be divided by our little partial interests; our projects will be confounded; and we ourselves shall become a reproach and a byword down to future ages. And what is worse, mankind may hereafter from this unfortunate instance despair of establishing governments by human wisdom and leave it to chance, war, and conquest.[10]

Indeed, it was not just republican government that would suffer from disunion; the likely result would be chaos and civil war. Gouverneur Morris of Pennsylvania looked into the fragmented future and gloomily observed that "the scenes of horror attending civil commotion cannot be described."[11]

In their early contributions to *The Federalist Papers*, the classic essays written in support of constitutional ratification in New York, John Jay and Alexander Hamilton elaborated on this prediction. We tend not to read these early essays today, focusing instead on the later analyses that help to illumine different features or provisions of the Constitution. But Jay and Hamilton attempted to motivate their readers from the outset by describing the appalling consequences of the imminent disunion they foresaw. Commercial rivalries and disputes over the vast and rich Western territories would lead to more violent conflicts. Larger states would attempt to gobble up smaller states. Smaller states would defend themselves by forming alliances with European powers. In sum, Alexander Hamilton predicted, the states would incur the consequences of "precisely the same inducements which have, at various times, deluged in blood all the nations in the world."[12] "These are not vague inferences drawn from speculative defects," he argued, but rather "solid conclusions drawn from the natural and necessary progress of human affairs."[13]

Maintenance of the nation, in short, was not just something that would be good for business, or for the politically ambitious. It was rather a necessary condition of republican government, here and elsewhere, now and in the future, and also a measure required to avert chaos and bloody civil strife. This was a frequent theme among the Philadelphia delegates.

Without appreciating this motivation on the part of the framers, we will not understand how and why they were able to do what they did—why they were able to achieve so much and also why they were ultimately willing, as we will see, to sacrifice even basic principles of justice to secure what they viewed as a higher good.

THE IMPOSSIBLE DREAM? CREATING A NATION

So it was imperative to hold the union together (or, if you prefer, to bring it into existence). That was no small task. We might say that the framers faced two kinds of daunting challenges—one technical, the other political.

The technical challenge was to fashion a legal framework that would support a central government with the powers characteristic of a *nation* (as opposed to a mere league of independent sovereigns, akin to today's United Nations) and yet would prevent that government from sacrificing or infringing the liberty for which Americans had just finished fighting their desperate war for independence. Given the framers' generally pessimistic views about men's inexorable drive to amass and abuse power, this was a formidable task just in itself.

And yet it was also necessary to confront the political challenge: no matter how masterful or elegant the frame of governance might be, the framers' efforts would be useless unless their proposal were something that their fellow citizens could be persuaded to accept. Fresh off a revolution fought against an oppressive foreign government, suspicious of anything that presented even a hint or possibility of overreaching authority, most Americans were not eager to create a new, distant, powerful central government. Unlike Madison, they were not devoting their days to contemplating abstruse matters like the long-term fate of republican government; they were busy plowing their fields and planting and harvesting their crops, working, worshiping, marrying, raising children. And the relatively few Americans who *were* involved in government, either in the national Congress or in the state legislatures, might naturally be disinclined to welcome a new government that would displace them or reduce their power. So there was understandably no swelling national consensus in favor of a complete overhaul of existing political arrangements.

And so the Philadelphia delegates faced two formidable challenges. And of course to make matters even more daunting, they needed to deal with the technical and political challenges simultaneously. It would be one thing—one seemingly almost impossible thing—to construct a frame of government that would preserve national unity while avoiding infringements of freedom. It would be another seemingly almost impossible thing to design a new government that would win the approval of a disparate collection of diverse and often contentious and ornery Americans. But to come up with a new government that would do both? Seriously?

So, how did the framers manage to accomplish this desperately difficult task? In our celebratory tellings (which, once again, contain a good measure of truth), we recall legendary, almost Herculean human figures and qualities—the unparalleled gravitas of Washington; the ambition and indefatigable brilliance of Hamilton; the uncanny combination of theoretical sophistication and backroom political savvy of Madison. Another part of the traditional story acknowledges the role of sheer good luck (or, as the delegates themselves insisted, Providence[14]). Although the Philadelphia convention was packed with luminaries, there were also major political figures, forceful and opinionated, who would likely have wrecked the convention—Thomas Jefferson, Patrick Henry, John Adams—but fortuitously were not in attendance. And we can see in retrospect that the Constitution was conceived and ratified during a narrow historical window in which such a project was possible. If the convention had met a year or two earlier, conditions and events (such as Shays's Rebellion) that would motivate Americans to consider drastic change were still in the future. If the convention had occurred two or three years later, conversely, after the French Revolution broke out, the bitter divisions provoked by that seismic struggle would almost certainly have precluded agreement here on any new frame of government.[15]

All of these edifying recollections may be true enough, but they do not yet answer the question on the ground. Granted that the Philadelphia delegates were an able bunch of men and that they enjoyed the favor of Fortune or Providence, still, how did they deal with the daunting technical and political challenges we have noted above?

Primarily, it seems, they focused on the technical challenge. So they devoted their discussions and energies to crafting a new national government that would have the power to defend the nation against foreign attacks or domestic insurrections, to tax and spend, to act directly on citizens, to energetically represent the collectivity in foreign affairs, to honor the nation's debts and obligations, and to sustain a unified national economy not disrupted by local discriminatory taxes and protectionist measures. At the same time, applying what they believed to be the lessons of modern political science, they also tried to constrain the powers of this new government—to prevent "tyranny," as they often called it—by employing the novel ideas of separation of powers, enumerated powers, and checks and balances in their framework.

The discussions thus primarily focused on nitty-gritty matters of institutional design and legal implementation. How many legislators should there be, and how should they be chosen, and by whom, and for what terms? What powers should be entrusted to the legislature, and should those powers be described in general terms or by means of an itemized list? How should the executive branch be structured—with a multi-person council, or a single executive? And how should that executive be selected? By the people? By the Congress? And for what term? Three years? Four years? Seven years? Should national officials be removable, and if so how and through what processes? Should new states be admitted to the union, and on what conditions and terms? And so on, and so on.

It was to such important but mundane questions that the delegates devoted their hours and days. The discussions were technical, and legalistic, and they produced a legalistic document that reflected those discussions. The delegates hoped (and argued, in the ratifying process) that they had managed to craft a frame of governance for a nation—with a central government possessing the powers characteristic of a nation—but in accordance with principles that would prevent that government from threatening the nation's newly acquired liberty.

But although their efforts were and needed to be addressed primarily to these technical questions, the delegates were also constantly aware of the political challenge, and the political constraints. Early in the deliberations, Pierce Butler of South Carolina admonished that "we must follow the example of Solon, who gave the Athenians not the best government he could devise, but the best they would receive."[16] The admonition was repeated on a regular, almost daily basis.

THE UNPRINCIPLED CONSTITUTION

The imperative of achieving general acceptance meant that no one could seriously expect to get the kind of constitution that he would have wanted—or that he would have believed to be in accord with justice and sound political principles. The delegates came to realize, rather, that in some important matters of principle, Americans held (and for the foreseeable future would continue to hold) fundamentally antagonistic views. Consequently, a constitution that would have any hope of uniting the nation would not only have to refrain from committing itself to any uplifting but contested and hence polarizing principles; it would have to deliberately neglect or overtly compromise such principles. In short, fundamental principles of justice would have to be sacrificed for the presumably greater good of national unity.

Some of the delegates—including some that we most admire—found it difficult to make this sacrifice. Some found it impossible. Sometimes the gut-twisting, conscience-searing compromises could only be achieved through stratagems or coverups: a morally intractable issue might need to be referred to a committee that could then work behind a veil of secrecy to cobble together a necessary but unseemly compromise, anonymously, so to speak, and phrased in terms of euphemisms then to be approved by delegates voting not in their own names but under the cover of their respective states.

Collectively, though, the delegates managed to rise to the challenge. Let us be blunt: they managed to muster up the fortitude—the strength of character, if you like—to betray their most basic political principles. They betrayed or at least bracketed those principles in order to create a thoroughly compromised frame of governance—one that could bring a differently-minded, diversely-oriented people together as a nation.

This is not the kind of Constitution that modern constitutionalists have wanted to embrace (as we will see in the following chapters). They have wanted a Constitution more pure and fulsome in its embrace of moral principles. But the framers' goal was to create a nation, and strengthening or constructing a union through the affirmation of grand or noble principles was plainly not part of their strategy.

Thus, beginning in May of 1787, discussions at the Philadelphia convention were shaped by a draft proposal known as the Virginia Plan. This proposal was basically an outline for the organizational structure of a new government; it did not contain any recitation of abstract principles or ideals. In the middle of June, small state delegates who were dissatisfied with the course of the discussions countered with their own proposal, or with what is called the New Jersey Plan. This proposal was likewise devoted to governmental organization, and was bereft of grand statements of principle.

Late in the convention, a committee on detail consolidated the various matters that had been agreed upon into a draft constitution—which again contained no affirmations of basic principles. A proposal *was* floated to adopt a bill of rights, as most state constitutions did. Such a measure might conceivably have contained statements of principle. But the proposal for a bill of rights was summarily rejected.

Thanks apparently to Gouveneur Morris's tinkering in a committee on style,[17] the final product did contain one eloquent sentence—the Preamble ("We the People . . . ")—that *can* be read as a statement of ideals. That sentence is important, and we will say more about it in due course. Even so, it was . . . one sentence—and pretty much an afterthought.

The absence of affirmations of principle becomes more starkly conspicuous if we compare the American Constitution with the one adopted almost contemporaneously in France. Thus, in 1789, the same year that the new American government commenced, the French revolutionaries adopted (with Jefferson's help) a visionary Declaration of the Rights of Man, which was crammed with grand ideals and principles. The Declaration began by asserting that "[m]en are born equal and free in rights. Social distinctions can be founded only on the common good." And the Declaration proceeded to spread out a virtual cornucopia of human rights, interlarded with fulsome expressions of noble ideals. ("All the citizens, being equal in its [the law's] eyes, are equally admissible to all public dignities, places, and employments, according to their capacity and without distinction other than that of their virtues and of their talents.") When shortly thereafter the French adopted a constitution, the document led off by incorporating this edifying Declaration.

The American Constitution, by contrast, contained nothing of this sort. Comparing the American and French constitutions, a detached observer might wonder: were the American founders somehow deficient in vision or moral commitment? Nose-to-the-grindstone political operatives, perhaps, lacking in larger ideas and ideals?

Any such assessment would be radically mistaken. In fact, as we will see, the founders did have strong commitments to ideas of justice and political morality; and they often expressed these commitments in the convention. But they evidently did not think it was the function of the Constitution itself to affirm such ideals. The Constitution had a different purpose. It was not to be a philosophical statement, or an edifying document, or a set of grand promises, but rather a legal instrument establishing the organizational framework for a new government. Even more sobering: the founders came to understand that in order to achieve their unifying purpose, it would not be enough to *refrain from declaring* the lofty but controversial principles they held dear. On the contrary: they would be called upon to *sacrifice and betray*—or at least to bracket and compromise—those principles.

THE CONSTITUTION OF COMPROMISE

Betraying basic principle: this was a grim necessity that the delegates did not appreciate at the outset. They began, rather, with the hope that the Constitution, while perhaps not explicitly *affirming* the principles of the recent revolution, would at least be *consistent with* those principles—and in particular with the revolutionary commitments to liberty, equality, and governance by the consent of the governed. And yet even their desire to keep the Constitution consistent with fundamental principles had to be subordinated to their primary goal—namely, to preserve or create a union, or a nation. This goal called upon the delegates to accept compromises, on matters both small and large.

Virtually every provision in the Constitution reflected some sort of compromise arising out of, and seeking to resolve, disagreement. Some of these disagreements look relatively small in retrospect, although they seemed weighty at the time. Should future censuses (by which, as the population changed, the states' representation in Congress would be adjusted) be mandated on a fixed schedule, or should the scheduling be left to future Congresses? Should the judiciary include lower federal courts in addition to the Supreme Court, or should cases instead be allowed to meander their way up to the Supreme Court by means of the state court systems? Should members of Congress be eligible to accept work in the executive branch? On these and countless other matters, sometimes strident disagreements broke out—and were resolved by compromise.

Even so, these were minor matters, relatively speaking. Mostly practical matters. But the delegates also disagreed on two enormous issues that they regarded as matters of fundamental justice. First, they disagreed about the nature or character of the government they were creating; and this disagreement was in turn reflective of fundamental disagreements about the source of political authority and the nature of political community—even, we might say, about the nature of human personhood. Second, they disagreed about slavery.

These disagreements were over principles so fundamental that many of the delegates believed—and insisted, emphatically and eloquently—that they were beyond compromise. Better that the nation fall apart than that principles so basic and so sacred be sacrificed.

And yet, somehow, compromises were achieved. By now we take those compromises for granted. But at least for some delegates the process of compromise was difficult, even morally anguished.

Representation and Legitimacy

Most Americans will recall learning that the Philadelphia convention ran into difficulties over the question of representation. Some delegates—mostly those from large and populous states like Pennsylvania or Virginia—thought that states should be represented in Congress in proportion to their respective populations. If Pennsylvania had three times as many citizens as New Jersey, Pennsylvania should get three times as many representatives. Other delegates, especially those from the smaller states, thought that each state should receive equal representation: for every representative from Pennsylvania, New Jersey should also have a representative. After debating this issue, the convention ended up splitting the difference by making the states' representation proportionate to population in the House of Representatives but equal in the Senate: we often refer to this deal as "the Great Compromise," or "the Connecticut Compromise."

This description is accurate enough as far as it goes. But it fails to reveal how deep the opposing commitments were—how deeply philosophical, we might say—and thus how resistant to compromise; and it also fails to appreciate how the resulting compromise rendered the document, and the new government, essentially and purposefully unprincipled and incoherent with respect to fundamental questions such as the source of political authority and the nature of the new political community. Nor was this purposeful incoherence limited to the particular feature of representation in Congress; it characterized the overall document—and the new government.

One way the fundamental disagreement could be and often was described (though not, I will suggest, the most perspicuous way) went like this: Was the new government to be a "national" government representing "the people," or rather a confederated or "federal" government representing "the states"?[18] The proponents of proportionate representation favored the former answer. And on that assumption, they concluded that a government based on equal representation of states would not merely be contrary to the interests of large states, or even unjust and unfair to those states. Such a government, they suggested, would be illegitimate in its very foundation—lacking in legitimate authority.

The point was perhaps most clearly put by Pennsylvania's James Wilson. Political authority, Wilson insisted, must come from "the legitimate source of authority"—namely, the people.[19] And it logically followed, he thought, that "as all authority was derived from the people, equal numbers of people ought to have an equal number of representatives, and different numbers of people ought to have different numbers of representatives."[20] Conversely, a government with representation based on something other than population—or "the people"—would not merely be inexpedient or unfair; it would be fundamentally illegitimate.

Other delegates—James Madison, Alexander Hamilton, Rufus King—embraced Wilson's logic. Their conviction that proportionate representation was required by fundamental principles of authority or legitimacy led these delegates to insist that their position simply could not be compromised. Why compromise if the result will be a government that is illegitimate? Rather than betray the most elemental principle of political authority, therefore, they were prepared to let the convention, and the nation, fall apart. In this spirit, Wilson declared defiantly that if delegates from states like New Jersey or Delaware or Maryland "refuse to coalesce with the majority on just and proper principles, if a separation must take place, it could never happen on better grounds."[21] King, Madison, and Hamilton concurred.

But were the proportionalists begging the question—assuming what was at issue? If the new government was to be a national one representing the American people, then Wilson's logic might seem unanswerable. Conversely, if the new government were conceived as a confederation of *states*, or of separate sovereigns (like NATO, say, or the UN), might it not seem logical that each sovereign should enjoy equal representation? In this vein, Luther Martin of Maryland replied that "an equal vote in each state . . . was founded in justice and freedom, not merely in policy."[22] These small state delegates agreed with Wilson and Madison and company that it would be better for the convention to fail rather than to create a new government on unjust principles. But they disagreed about what those principles were.

To this position, though, the proportionalists had a response—one that seemed to them utterly compelling. Once again, political authority is to be based on the "consent of the governed." This was an "unalienable truth" that was declared in the Declaration of Independence as a premise for the revolution, wasn't it? And the governed are "the people." It is *people* for whom governments are organized, not *states*.

Indeed, states were not even quite real; they were more in the nature of "metaphysical" abstractions, Wilson argued, or "imaginary beings."[23] In the same vein, Alexander Hamilton contended that states were mere "artificial beings," or "collections of individual men." And "[n]othing could be more preposterous or absurd"—Hamilton was not a man given to subtlety or understatement—than to fashion a government based on representation of the "artificial beings" rather than the real entities, or the "individual men."[24]

Massachusetts delegate and Harvard-educated lawyer Rufus King agreed. Expressing his "amazement" that anyone could with a straight face defend a system in which it was states rather than people who were represented in Congress, King peremptorily dismissed the whole idea as a "wonderful illusion."[25]

In the face of this seemingly compelling position, the state-egalitarians (if we can call them that) seemed to take refuge in procedural technicalities. Thus, beyond simply declaring that their own states would never agree to ratify a document providing for proportionate representation,[26] their most frequent contention was that the delegates had been appointed *by their states*, as representatives *of those states*; and they had been appointed not to create a new frame of government, but rather to devise and propose reforms of the Articles of Confederation, under which states enjoyed equal representation. So the delegates and the convention simply had no authority to depart from the system of equal representation of states.[27]

Strictly speaking, the state-egalitarians were probably correct. In Federalist 40, Madison would devote so much energy and ingenuity to excusing and apologizing for the convention's disregard of its marching orders that one may be provoked to wonder whether he was suffering from a guilty conscience. And yet people who believe they have the *power* to do something noble and visionary are likely to chafe upon being told that, technically, they were never clearly given *authority* to do this wonderful new thing. So Madison and Wilson and others listened to the small states' *ultra vires* argument and in effect asked, "Is that the best you can do? Because if it is, then. . . . " And they naturally suspected—and sometimes explicitly *said*—that the small state delegates were hypocrites; they were in reality acting from self-interest (or from the interests of the states they represented) and were merely pretending to believe that equal state representation would be just.[28]

A modern reader of the debates might readily agree, in part because the Wilson-Madison position on representation resonates with modern views that have been officially endorsed by the Supreme Court in its voting rights decisions,[29] and in part because (meaning no disrespect to the other delegates) it seems not unfair to observe that Wilson and Madison were perhaps the most articulate and analytically gifted—and also the best prepared—of the delegates. And indeed, as long as the central question is phrased in the terms favored by the proportionalists—Is government for *people* or instead for constructed and "imaginary" entities like *states*?—the proportionalist position does seem almost irresistible.

So then, was the procedural, ultra vires argument the only one that the small state delegates could offer? It is hard to know. At one point late in the debates on the issue, James Wilson disdainfully asserted that no delegate had even tried to offer any cogent argument against the justice of proportional representation.[30] But of course we are mostly dependent for our knowledge of the debates on notes kept by Madison, who surely thought that the justice of his and Wilson's position was self-evident. So if any delegates did offer justice-based arguments for the opposing position, it is possible that Madison failed to record the arguments, or perhaps to understand them: after all, even astute people like Madison often have difficulty discerning the logic of a position that they firmly believe to be not only wrong but hypocritical and wicked.

Who Are (or Is) "the People"?

Whether or not the small state delegates succeeded in articulating their deeper normative assumptions, though, we can perhaps with some reflection excavate those assumptions. The Declaration of Independence had asserted that governmental authority must be based on "the consent of the governed." And "the governed," it seems, are "the people." Those propositions were the core of the proportionalists' case. And yet the state-egalitarians need not have quarreled with either of those propositions. At bottom, they might have explained, the underlying disagreement was not actually over "people vs. states." The real disagreement, rather, was over who or what "the people" is, or are. Proportionalists like Wilson and Madison were evidently taking for granted what we might call an atomistic conception of "the people," while the state-egalitarians were implicitly assuming a more communal conception.

Thus, in the Wilson-Madison view, what is real, and thus the source of political authority, is—or rather *are*—the individual human beings living within some region or jurisdiction. Obadiah Jones, Mary Anderson, Jeremiah Stout: these are "the people." The collective noun—"the people"—is merely a label for a class of individual human beings. So "We the People of . . ."

might be less elegantly but more precisely rendered as "We the *persons* living within...." And it is these persons—these individual human beings—whose consent is essential to political authority. By contrast, political units that these individuals may construct—going under names like Massachusetts, Pennsylvania, and so forth—are not even quite real: they are "metaphysical" or "imaginary," as Wilson said, or "artificial," as Hamilton put it.

State-egalitarians might have responded, however, that for all of its surface clarity, and despite what proportionalists took to be its self-evident quality, this conception of "the people" and of the political communities called "states" was far from mandatory. Indeed, they might have gone farther and contended that the atomistic conception was naively reductionist, and that the proportionalists' dismissals of the states as "artificial" or "imaginary" was facile.

Thus, it might well be that an entity like "New Jersey" is an "imaginary being" in the sense that it exists in part in people's imaginations. An admired modern study explains that political communities are indeed "imagined"[31]: what makes something a "community" is not the mere existence of a collection of individual human beings living in geographical proximity to each other, but rather the fact that these human beings think of themselves—or *imagine themselves*—as a community. Something similar might be said about a great many other important things: a political movement (like Communism, or the Civil Rights movement), a world religion (like Christianity or Judaism), an economic system (like the American economy), a legal system (like "the common law"), a business enterprise (like IBM, or AT&T), an academic discipline (like sociology, or philosophy). These things are not just collections of material or empirically observable facts. Rather, they exist—exist *as entities*, as *real* entities—because people *believe* them to be real entities and act in accordance with that belief. Such things are no less "real" for being "constructed"—the Hoover Dam is constructed, after all, but it is surely real—or for subsisting, in part, in people's imaginations.

Neither does their partly imaginary or imagined quality make such entities unworthy of respect—or perhaps, in the proper context, of representation. They are deserving of respect or representation not in their own right, we might say, but rather because and insofar as the human beings who compose and construct them (in part by imagining them) *believe* them to be deserving of respect and representation. So if a group of people living in a particular locale conceive of themselves as having a common and constitutive connection, and if they conceive of this connection under the heading of "New Jersey," and if these people feel affection and loyalty to the (imagined but nonetheless real community of) New Jersey, then it makes no sense to say that we should give respect to these "individual men" but not to "New Jersey."

In withholding respect (or representation) for "New Jersey," we withhold respect (or representation) for the "individual men" as well.[32]

Indeed, from the communal perspective, the distinction between "individual men" and "the state" is a false and misleading dichotomy. And in assuming and insisting on that dichotomy, Hamilton and Wilson and Madison were doing violence to the reality. The state of New Jersey, after all, is not something separate and apart from the "individual men" who help to constitute it. Conversely, what is it that constitutes the "individual men"—John James, Mary Stout, Jeremiah Stockwell—as the persons they are, or that gives them their substance and identity as "individual men"? A variety of things, probably; but their relation to other people and things (including to "imagined communities," like, say, New Jersey) will be essential ingredients.

So we approach an "individual man" and ask: "Who are you? Tell us who you are. Not just your name: that means us little or nothing to us. Tell us who *you* really are." The man is likely to respond by describing a set of relations to people or collective entities. "I'm the son of Gladys and Herbert. I'm a die hard Yankees fan—season ticket holder for the last thirty years. I'm a deacon in the Presbyterian church, and a member of the Rotary Club." And for many people, a relation to a political entity may well figure on this list, even centrally or prominently. "I'm a Virginian." Or "I'm an American." Peel off this political relation and we are no longer understanding—or accurately representing—the "individual man."

On this more communal conception, to render "We the People of . . . " as "We the *individual persons* living in . . . " is to lose the vital and valuable meaning of the phrase. "We the People" refers to a *communal* entity, composed to be sure of human beings—but human beings understood in relation to and as partly constituted by their relation to a political community. And it is that communal entity—"The People"—that is "the governed" whose consent is the basis of political authority.

So to Wilson's and Hamilton's contention that a government based on representation of states rather than "individual men" would lack legitimacy, because not based on "the source of legitimacy," the state-egalitarians might have turned the argument around. The difficulty of explaining authority as the product of consent by the myriad persons or "individual men" is notorious, among both philosophers and non-philosophers: the plain fact is that most "individual men" have *not* given their consent, and indeed were never even asked to give it. And expedients like "implied consent" or "constructive consent" seem painfully contrived.[33] On the atomistic account of "the people," in short, political authority and hence "legitimacy" seem doomed. It is only if "We the People" is understood in a more communal sense that some kind of "consent" might plausibly be ascribed to them—or rather to *it*.

Thus, although the proportionalists and the state-egalitarians might have agreed in affirming that political authority should be based on "the consent of the governed," or on the consent of "We the People," they talked past each other because they were working from fundamentally different conceptions of who "the people" was (or were), or of how "the people" was (or were) constituted. To pose the question as "the people versus the states?," was to finesse the vital question, which in fact went something like this: "Is the new government to be conceived of as a government of the people-regarded-as-separate-individuals, or rather of the people-regarded-in-relation-to-their-constitutive-communities? (Or some combination thereof?) Framed in this way, the question is not rhetorical, as Wilson and Hamilton supposed, but is very much a debatable question.

In sum, each side advocated a system of representation that was consonant with justice as they conceived it; and each side believed that a government not based on such representation would be fundamentally unjust and indeed illegitimate. It was hardly surprising, therefore, that delegates on each side repeatedly insisted that they were prepared to see the convention collapse, and the nation fall apart, rather than endorse a new government based on wrong and unjust principles.

THE PAINFUL RETREAT FROM PRINCIPLE

And yet the convention did not collapse, and the nation did not fall apart. So, how did the delegates manage to achieve a compromise that could reconcile such antagonistic views?

With effort and reflection and deliberation, the delegates managed, if not actually to agree, at least to acknowledge their fallibility and to respect the views and principles of their opponents. Right?

Not quite. There were to be sure advocates of compromise, and also conciliatory figures, such as Benjamin Franklin, who pleaded with the delegates to admit that they might be mistaken, as a step toward the acceptance of compromise.[34] And yet throughout the convention, the more articulate and forceful delegates on each side of the issue showed no signs of acknowledging that they might be wrong, or that there might be merit in the opposing position. Rather, they tended to view their opponents as acting from self-interest in disregard of manifestly correct principles.

When reasoning failed to bring unity, Franklin attempted a more spiritual strategy. Remarking that the convention was "groping . . . in the dark to find political truth," he proposed that the convention institute a practice of daily prayer, "humbly applying to the Father of Lights to illuminate our understandings."[35] The proposal was summarily rebuffed. Understandably so: why would you petition heaven for light and guidance when the truth was already perfectly clear, and the problem was just that some people refused out of pure pigheaded self-interest to accept it? Wouldn't it be hypocritical to pretend to ask the Almighty a question when you already know what the answer has to be?

Compromise was achieved, rather, through procedural maneuvering reinforced by an awareness of the awful consequences of failure. Thus, when the debate over representation had reached an impassioned impasse, Roger Sherman proposed to refer the question to a committee. The evident purpose of this move, as the composition of the committee would reflect, was to devise a compromise[36]—mostly likely one similar to the compromise Sherman had already proposed at an earlier stage.[37] And indeed, some delegates were already insisting on the need for compromise. "If no compromise should take place," predicted Oliver Ellsworth of Connecticut, "our meeting would not only be in vain but worse than in vain."[38] "Something must be done," Elbridge Gerry pleaded, "or we shall disappoint not only America but the whole world."[39]

Fully cognizant of what was going on and unwilling to compromise on principle, the astute Madison opposed the referral to committee.[40] But the referral was approved over his objection. And after recessing to celebrate Independence Day (and perhaps thereby renewing their commitment to saving the nation from disintegration), the delegates reconvened on July 5 and received the committee's report. As expected, this report proposed in essence the compromise that we have lived with ever since—namely, equal representation of states in the Senate, proportional representation in the House. (Apparently as a concession to the large state delegates, the compromise also provided that tax bills needed to originate in the proportionally constituted House, although Wilson and Madison and others scoffed at this ostensible sop thrown to them.[41])

But those who believed proportional representation to be required by fundamental principles of justice continued to oppose this measure, vociferously. James Wilson asked rhetorically: "What hopes will our Constituents entertain when they find that the essential principles of justice have been violated at the outset of the Government."[42] Rufus King asked: "What reason can be assigned why the same rule of representation should not prevail in the second branch as in the first? He could conceive of none." And King went on to argue that "no Government could last that was not founded on just principles," and that it would be better to do nothing, and "to submit to a little more confusion and convulsion, that to submit to such an evil."[43] Madison gave a lengthy speech opposing a government based on "improper principles" and arguing that under the proposed compromise "the proper foundation of Government was destroyed."[44]

With respect to the conciliatory claim that the new government would be "partly national, partly federal," Madison systematically deconstructed this characterization. The description would make sense, he said, only if the new government would in some respects act directly on citizens and in other respects on states. But there were no ways in which the government would act directly on states.[44,45] So the "part federal, part national" slogan made no sense; it was nonsense.

Over these objections, the convention nonetheless swung in favor of the committee's proposal. The majority sentiment did not defend the compromise against Wilson's and Madison's objections of injustice and incoherence, but rather concluded that even an unprincipled compromise was better than national disintegration. "If no Accommodation takes place," urged Caleb Strong of Massachusetts, "the Union itself must soon be dissolved."[46] "If no compromise take place," Elbridge Gerry concurred, "what will be the consequence? A secession."[47] Gouverneur Morris of Pennsylvania elaborated: "This country must be united. If persuasion does not unite it, the sword will."[48]

Those with strong convictions, including Wilson and Madison, still could not bring themselves to endorse the compromise. And Wilson's and Madison's resistance prevailed within their state delegations. Thus, Pennsylvania and Virginia continued to vote "no" on the compromise.[49] And when the measure was narrowly adopted over their objection, they seriously contemplated terminating the convention. Observing that it would be difficult to go forward on unacceptable foundations, Edmund Randolph offered what sounded like a motion for final adjournment. William Patterson eagerly responded that "if Mr. Randolph would reduce to form his motion for an adjournment sine die, he [Patterson] would second it with all his heart." After a rebuke and warning from General Pinckney, however, these delegates backtracked: Randolph protested that "his meaning had been . . . strangely misunderstood"—he had meant to adjourn only until the following day, he now insisted—and Patterson seconded that much revised motion instead.[50]

Large state delegates used the temporary adjournment to meet and discuss how to proceed, but they failed to settle on a strategy. Madison's dejection and disgust are evident in his notes: "The time was wasted in vague conversation on the subject, without any specific proposition or agreement." The tone of his description leaves little doubt about what his own preferred strategy would have been. Thus, Madison reported that some delegates urged that the large states should form their own convention and propose their own constitution.

> No good Government could or would be built on that foundation [i.e. of the recently approved compromise], and . . . as a division of the Convention into

two opinions was unavoidable, it would be better that the side composing the principal States, and a majority of the of the people of America, should propose a scheme of Government to the States.

Does it sound like Madison is conveying his own view here? But "others seemed inclined to yield to the smaller States, and to concur in such an act however imperfect and exceptionable, as might be agreed on by the Convention as a body, though decided by a bare majority of States and by a minority of the people of the United States." As a result of this deadlock, Madison morosely observed, the smaller states probably perceived that they had nothing to fear from any combination of the large states in favor of just principles.[51]

And so despite their eloquent expositions of principle and their earnest protestations that no government could be formed on improper principles, Madison and Wilson and their colleagues acquiesced. They did not walk out of the convention. And in the end, they put their names to the final product. Then they went back to their states and vigorously campaigned for its adoption.

Did they actually come to see the wisdom or value of the compromise that they had so vehemently opposed? Maybe, maybe not. In Federalist 39, Madison offered a lengthy analysis of the diverse ways in which the new government was variously "federal" (ratification, composition of the Senate, limited national powers) "national" (composition of the House of Representatives, operation of national powers directly on citizens), and mixed (selection of the President, constitutional amendments); and he concluded that "[t]he proposed Constitution . . . is, in strictness, neither a national nor a federal Constitution, but a composition of both."[52] Was Madison thus commending as a virtue the compromise that he had in convention strenuously condemned as incoherent and unjust?

Perhaps. Joseph Ellis argues that Madison left the convention in despair but then through reflection came to appreciate the virtues of compromises that he had previously opposed.[53] And it is easy to read his analysis in Federalist 39 as a commendation of the "partly federalist, partly nationalist" government, coming as the analysis does as part of an essay urging adoption of the Constitution. And yet, closely examined, the essay appears to be neutrally descriptive; it contains no explicit praise of the arrangement. And just two essays earlier, in Federalist 37, Madison had explained how compromise had been unavoidable, and how precisely on this point of representation "the convention must have been compelled to sacrifice theoretical propriety to the force of extraneous considerations."[54] "[A] faultless plan was not to be expected," he observed, concluding philosophically that it could only be attributable to Providence that the convention had managed to surmount so many disagreements and difficulties in order to reach agreement on a proposal.[55] Madison, it seems, now accepted the compromise as necessary, and he was willing to present it in the most favorable light. But he still did not go so far as actually to commend it.

This fundamental disagreement—over political authority and the nature of the new political community—manifested itself not only in the question of representation but in other contexts as well. The same basic disagreement, and the same basic compromise, reappeared in discussions and decisions about the selection of the President. Thus, the electoral college, in which each state would receive a number of electors based on the sum of its representatives and senators, reflected the compromise view in which both the individual citizens and the states would be constitutive components of the new government. And although an earlier draft of the preamble that had listed the various states as the authors of the constitution was later amended to delete the states in favor of "We the People of the United States," the individual states were still acknowledged in Article VII. The Constitution was to be ratified, in other words, not by "We the People of the United States," but rather by the people of New York, and the people of Virginia, and the people of each state individually. And it was to be binding only upon states that so ratified.

And so, failing to resolve their disagreement over the nature of the new government but determined to avoid fragmentation and potential civil war, the delegates sent out to the nation—or rather to the various states—an incoherent design proposal for a government that would be "part national, part federal." The state conventions likewise argued about the issue, and likewise failed to resolve the disagreement, and likewise eventually brought themselves to ratify the incoherent proposal. They did so for basically the same reason that the convention did: they perceived that it would be better to sacrifice political principles than to descend into disorder and chaos.

In the ensuing decades, this incoherence in the new government would surface again and again, as specific disagreements (over Supreme Court jurisdiction, for example, or tariffs, or slavery) would arise and partisans of the different views would raise the same basic opposing arguments that the Philadelphia delegates had pressed and had failed to reconcile. Nor was this disagreement ever resolved by argument. It was resolved, eventually, only by a horrific war. And even then the resolution was hardly final, or secure: a "partly national, partly federal" government continues to plague us—or perhaps to bless us, but in any case to hold us uneasily together—to this day.

Considering how much passion has been spent and how much blood spilled over this disagreement, we might be tempted to look back and castigate the framers for not settling the issue, one way or the other, at the outset. But such recriminations would be misguided. The fact was that the issue *could not* be resolved. Insistence on a principled resolution would only have precluded ratification, thereby producing disunity and perhaps civil war at an earlier stage and on a more frequent basis. The framers' willingness to compromise in effect bought the nation seven decades of (often fractious) unity before the Civil War occurred.

And when it did occur, of course, that war was not merely the product of disagreement over the nature of the union, or of "the people." It was even more closely and intensely related to the other enormous issue that the framers also failed to resolve—namely, slavery.

COMPROMISING ON SLAVERY

The challenge to the Philadelphia convention posed by slavery differed in two fundamental respects from the challenge posed by representation. In the first place, although the convention plainly needed to specify how representation in the new government would work, it did not obviously need to say or do anything about slavery. In 1787, slavery flourished in some states, and it had already been abolished in other states. The convention had been called not to address the issue of slavery, but rather to do something about the organization and powers of the central government. In theory, the delegates might have constructed a plan for a new national government without saying anything about slavery one way or the other, thus leaving the institution as it already was.

And indeed, some of the delegates—many of them, probably—would surely have preferred just to leave the matter alone. But this option proved to be unavailable for two principal reasons. Insofar as representation in the House of Representatives would be based on population, the convention needed to decide whether or not slaves would count as persons for representation purposes. For understandable reasons, southern states wanted slaves to be counted for this purpose (thereby increasing their populations and hence their representation); northern delegates did not. Second, fearing that a strengthened national government might act to restrict slavery or the slave trade, representatives of southern states demanded protections for their "peculiar institution." As Pierce Butler of South Carolina explained, "[t]he security the southern states want is that their Negroes may not be taken from them, which some gentlemen within or without doors have a very good mind to do."[56]

And so it turned out that, as the deliberations proceeded, the matter of slavery could not be passed over in silence. Even so, in understanding what the convention did, it is important to recall that the convention was not called on and did not attempt actually to resolve the fundamental question of the legality or morality of slavery on the merits.

Insofar as they did speak to that question, though, the delegates largely agreed in regarding the institution as unjust and inconsistent with the principles of the revolution. (They thus provided the raw material for interpreting the Constitution either as hypocritical or as a source of promises to be "redeemed.") Some of the delegates issued passionate denunciations, as we will see; the denouncers included delegates from southern states, even including at least one slaveholder (George Mason). Conversely, there was little effort to justify slavery as a just or moral institution. At one point, Charles Pinckney of South Carolina offered what seems to have been a halfhearted defense: slavery had been practiced throughout history, he said, including by "Greece, Rome, and other ancient states," as well as by modern nations including "France, England, Holland." But Pinckney also professed himself personally opposed to slavery, and he predicted that if left to themselves, Southern states would probably end up eliminating it.[57]

The issue of slavery was difficult, therefore—and this is the second main difference from the representation issue—not so much because it involved a conflict of fundamental principles, but rather because the institution was so entrenched and so indispensable that delegates of southern states affirmed, over and over again, that they and their states could never approve the new Constitution unless protections for slavery were included. Conversely, at least a few delegates protested that they could never support a Constitution that gave such protection. And so, once again, the excruciating moral question was presented: could a commitment to a principle as fundamental as human freedom—and, as we would say, "human dignity"—be compromised in order to maintain the unity of the nation?

With respect to the question of counting slaves for purposes of representation, the delegates seem not to have anguished overmuch. The question was settled with the now infamous "three-fifths compromise": for purposes of representation, a slave would be counted as three-fifths of a person. In 1787, this compromise did not provoke the sort of moral indignation that we today might think it deserved. There was opposition to the compromise, to be sure, along with charges of inconsistency. Southerners, it was objected, wanted slaves to count as persons for purposes of national representation even though slaves were not so counted in the states themselves.[58] And how could Southerners contend that slaves were persons for one purpose (representation) but were property for other purposes? Gouverneur Morris also registered a more substantive objection—not to slavery itself, exactly, but to the slave trade: he declared that "he could never agree to give such encouragement to the slave trade as would be given by allowing [Southern states] a representation for their Negroes."[59]

For the most part, though, the convention seemed to regard the issue not so much as a matter of principle but rather as a technical matter of fixing a formula of representation. Slaves were persons but they were also property: so counting them as three-fifths in the formula seemed acceptable. In fairness, no one suggested that an African slave was actually in some sense morally equivalent to three-fifths of a white person—although the delegates' resort to wording that carefully avoided using the terms "slave" or "slavery" may be indicative of a guilty conscience.

By contrast to the three-fifths compromise, the measures designed to insulate slavery and the slave trade against national regulation *were* perceived by some as accepting and protecting, and thus as tacitly approving, the institution of slavery itself. And so the measures provoked strong protests by delegates who abhorred that institution. Roger Sherman condemned the slave trade as "iniquitous."[60] Gouverneur Morris said that slavery was "a nefarious institution" and "the curse of heaven on the states where it prevailed." Constitutional accommodations for slavery amounted to "a sacrifice of every principle of right, of every impulse of humanity." He himself "never would concur in upholding domestic slavery."[61] Rufus King "was not sure he could assent to it under any circumstances."[62] Luther Martin protested that "it was inconsistent with the principles of the revolution and dishonorable to the American character to have [protections for slavery] in the Constitution."[63] George Mason (himself a slaveholder) declaimed at length on the moral, cultural, economic, and political evils of slavery and declared that the institution would "bring the judgment of heaven on a country." His ominous prediction turned out to be prophetic: "By an inevitable chain of causes and effects, providence punishes national sins by national calamities."[64]

The response, once again, was simply that slavery was a necessary evil: southern states were so dependent on it that they would never approve the Constitution unless the institution were protected against national interference.[65] And in the end, this declaration (or this threat) proved decisive. As with the representation controversy, the issue provoked impassioned debate—and was then referred to a committee,[66] so that compromises could be approved later after emotions and rhetoric had calmed down. In the course of this deescalation, delegates like King and Morris, though they had previously indicated their unwillingness to compromise on the issue, were lulled into a quiet acquiescence. The prospect that the convention and the nation would fall apart was sufficiently dire, it seems, that they were willing to suspend or bracket their principles for the sake of national unity.

Compromise was made easier by the fact that the Constitution was not actually instituting slavery, or even explicitly approving it, but was merely omitting to end or interfere with it. Roger Sherman expressed a common sentiment:

> He disapproved of the slave trade, yet as the states were now possessed of the right to import slaves, as the public good did not require it to be taken from them, and as it was expedient to have as few objections as possible to the proposed scheme of government, he thought it best to leave the matter as we find it.[67]

As we know, later generations would deplore this arrangement. William Lloyd Garrison, for example, famously denounced the Constitution as "a pact with the devil." From our own vantage point, we might–and many do[68]–blame the framers for accepting such accommodations. We might wish that, to the contrary, the framers had risen to the moral challenge and abolished the institution. How much horrific injustice might have been avoided, how much violence and bloodshed might have been averted, if the framers had simply done at that time what had to wait decades for the Civil War and the Emancipation Proclamation and the Thirteenth and Fourteenth Amendments! How different, and how much more peaceful and admirable, our whole history might have been if the "original sin" of slavery had been expunged at the Republic's beginning.

But of course, if we condemn the framers for this ostensible failure, we blame them for not doing what they could not possibly have done. Insistence on abolition of slavery would surely have doomed any prospect for adoption of the new constitution, which barely passed anyway in several of the states.[69] Joseph Ellis observes that "slavery was, on the one hand, a cancerous tumor in the American body politic and, on the other, a malignancy so deeply embedded that it could not be removed without killing the patient."[70] A refusal to compromise would not have freed any slaves; instead, the Southern states would most likely have gone their own way, and hence would have been released to maintain and develop the institution without opposition from the North. There is no way to be sure, of course, but it seems likely that this course would have meant that slavery would have been preserved for an even longer period.

THE INSPIRATIONAL PREAMBLE

Our review thus far has depicted the Constitution as a technical, legalistic document that not only lacked affirmations of fundamental principles but that deliberately rejected or at least compromised such principles. And yet principles or ideals are not altogether absent from the Constitution. There is after all the eloquent Preamble.

We the People of the United States, in Order to form a more perfect Union, establish Justice, insure domestic Tranquility, provide for the common defence, promote the general Welfare, and secure the Blessings of Liberty to ourselves and our Posterity, do ordain and establish this CONSTITUTION for the United States of America.

This statement, as we have seen, was not part of the Virginia Plan, or of the New Jersey Plan, or of the constitution returned late in the convention by the committee on detail. That document had instead begun with a much less exhilarating preamble: "We the people of the States of New Hampshire, Massachusetts . . . South-Carolina, and Georgia, do ordain, declare, and establish the following Constitution for the Government of Ourselves and our Posterity."[71] Evidently Gouveneur Morris inserted the more idealistic language—"a more perfect Union," "Justice," "the Blessings of Liberty"—as a late addition in the committee on style that prepared the final draft of the Constitution.[72]

This language endowed the document with at least a smattering of idealistic rhetoric or commitment. Indeed, perhaps the most idealistic part of the Preamble is actually the first phrase: "We the People of the United States. . . . " At the time, most Americans probably did not think of themselves as belonging to such an entity; they likely considered themselves to be constituents of "the People of Virginia," and of "Pennsylvania," and of their various states. So it seems fair to characterize these words as aspirational in character, and as consistent with what we have said the primary goal of the convention was—namely, to create a union or a nation.

In their desperate search for some textual basis for interpreting the Constitution as a repository of fundamental principles, later interpreters have naturally gravitated to the Preamble (and also to the Declaration of Independence). This reliance seems justified up to a point: the language does show that the framers were cognizant of—and were motivated by—ideals and principles, such as "Justice" and the "General Welfare." As we have already observed, that was why they thought it so imperative to establish a "more perfect Union" and to preserve republican government.

And yet if we are seeking to understand the character of the Constitution, two features of the Preamble are conspicuous. First, the ideals are stated at such a level of abstraction that they could hardly be controversial. People have fought verbal and physical wars over their competing conceptions of justice, but (excepting the occasional cynical Thrasymachus) hardly anyone is opposed in principle to justice. What is noteworthy about the Preamble, one might observe, is not so much that it expresses approval of "Justice" but that it makes no attempt to specify what Justice is. Second, the phrasing of the Preamble suggests that it is intended not as an enforceable provision but merely as an introductory indication of general goals. And indeed, the Supreme Court has typically interpreted the language in that way.

The Preamble thus suggests the role of principles and ideals in the framers' constitutional strategy. The project is indeed motivated at one level by the desire to promote and achieve lofty ideals. Without such ideals, what would be the point? Why would citizens feel any allegiance to a political project bereft of ideals and principles? At the same time, understanding that citizens' interpretations of these ideals will differ, and that ideals have the potential to be divisive rather than unifying, the Constitution leaves the ideals both unspecified and unenforced. The ideals are a prelude to a *legal* document establishing a framework of governance. And that legal document, far from articulating enforceable principles, reflects a deliberate and pervasive strategy of *not resolving* disputes over or among principles on a constitutional level, and indeed of compromising them in the structures it establishes.

RISING ABOVE PRINCIPLES?

Modern constitutionalists are familiar with the fact that compromises were made in order to secure agreement on the new Constitution. But they often seem to overlook the fact that these compromises informed and pervaded the document that was agreed on—that unprincipled compromises were in a sense the essence of that Constitution. The Constitution, we might say, was the product of a self-conscious effort in bracketing, containing, or suspending fundamental principles. That is the kind of document that was created in order to bring America together as a nation, and to govern that nation.

Modern constitutionalists have sometimes found this unprincipled quality a source of regret or embarrassment, and as we will see in the next chapter, they have wanted to imagine—indeed, have insisted on imagining—that the Constitution is an altogether different kind of instrument. Something more like Justice Brennan's "sublime oration on the dignity of man." And modern constitutionalists have sometimes reproached the framers for their willingness to compromise or bracket their convictions on matters like slavery.

Is this attitude of reproach warranted?

In everyday life we often admire a man or woman "of principle"—someone who stays faithful to his or her principles even at the cost of adverse consequences. Martyrs who willingly die for their faith or their country are the culminating case, and they elicit our admiration.

And yet we also think there is such a thing as overscrupulosity. And our assessment may be different for situations in which a person's rigid adherence to principle will cause other people to suffer. The man who will not tell a lie or sacrifice a principle in order to save his family—or, in a standard example, to conceal Jews being sought out by the Gestapo—is not necessarily to be admired. On the contrary.

Compromise is at the core of politics, which is (as the saying goes) "the art of the possible." True, we may often think of politicians as too ready to compromise, as unprincipled, as opportunistic and sleazy. The descriptions may be accurate enough in many cases. Even so, politics for a diverse people is not possible without compromise—without a willingness to bend or bracket or suspend principles in order to achieve a greater good.

The framers were involved in politics, obviously, and they were seeking the greater good of national unity. How valuable a good was that? How great a sacrifice of principle would the good of national unity justify? Could it justify compromise even on a matter of principle as fundamental as slavery?

"Unity" sounds abstract, perhaps not especially compelling. The framers sometimes spelled it out in commercial terms: national unity would enable the creation of a great commercial empire. Weighed against the evil of slavery, that good may not elicit our sympathy. At other times the framers elaborated on unity in terms of peace: without unity, the states would likely degenerate into a multitude of warring rivals. Violence, bloodshed, hatred: these would be the price of disunity. Perhaps the moral balance begins to tip in the framers' favor.

Surely, though, there are injustices so serious, and incurred so directly, that not even national unity could be a sufficient justification. Suppose, for example, that national unity could be achieved only by the adoption of a deliberate policy of genocide with respect to some minority ethnic group. At that point, surely, the moral calculus would prescribe a sacrifice of unity in order to avoid an egregious moral wrong.

Or would it? What if the consequence of disunity would be war, in which the minority group (along with many other people) would likely be annihilated anyway?

These are hard questions—for ordinary human beings, for moral philosophers, for politicians who have not anesthetized their consciences. The American framers and founding generation answered the question that were presented to them by choosing, in some cases reluctantly, to bracket or compromise fundamental principles in order to create a nation. We may or may not approve of their choice. But we have inherited the benefits, and also the burdens, of that choice.

And we face analogous choices in our own time. We can appreciate—and perhaps learn from—their travails and achievements as we face these choices.

NOTES

1 We say "at least until very recently" because over just the last several years apocalyptic talk that was once confined to a tiny lunatic fringe– talk of civil war or secessionhas become more common. See, e.g., F. H. Buckley, *American Secession: The Looming Threat of a National Breakup* (New York: Encounter Books, 2020).

2 Justice William J. Brennan, Jr., "To the Text and Teaching Symposium, Georgetown University," speech, October 12, 1985, https://fedsoc.org/commentary/publications/the-great-debate-justice-william-j-brennan-jr-october-12-1985.

3 See Seth Stern and Stephen Wermeil, *Justice Brennan: Liberal Champion* (Boston, Houghton Mifflin Harcourt, 2010), 91.

4 Probably the most eloquent and developed version of this story is Jack Balkin, *Constitutional Redemption* (Cambridge: Harvard University Press, 2011).

5 Joseph J. Ellis, *The Quartet: Orchestrating the Second American Revolution, 1783–1789* (New York: Alfred A. Knopf, 2015).

6 Quoted in Ellis, *The Quartet*, 3.

7 Edward J. Larson and Michael P. Winship, *The Constitutional Convention: A Narrative History from the Notes of James Madison* (New York: Modern Library, 2005), 46–47.

8 Ibid., 57.

9 Ibid., 58.

10 Ibid., 63.

11 Ibid., 75.

12 Alexander Hamilton, "Federalist No. 7," in *The Federalist Papers*, ed. Clinton Rossiter (New York: Signet Classic, 2003).

13 Alexander Hamilton, "Federalist No. 8," in *The Federalist Papers*, 63.

14 See James Madison, "Federalist No. 37," in *The Federalist Papers*, 226–27 ("It is impossible for a man of pious reflection not to perceive in [the creation of the Constitution] a finger of that Almighty hand which has been so frequently and signally extended to our relief in the critical stages of the revolution.").

15 Bruce Ackerman, *We the People: Foundations*, Vol. 1 (Cambridge: Belknap Press of Harvard University Press), 169.

16 Larson and Winship, *The Constitutional Convention*, 30.

17 See Ellis, *The Quartet*, 151.

18 See, e.g., Larson and Winship, *The Constitutional Convention*, 43.

19 Ibid., 31. See also ibid., 34.

20 Ibid., 39.

21 Ibid., 69. See also ibid., 39.

22 Ibid., 60. And Roger Sherman of Connecticut argued that in most states poor voters and rich voters usually got one vote apiece, even though the rich voters paid more taxes than the poorer voters did. This equal distribution of voting rights "arises from an equal distribution of liberty among all ranks." Sherman thought that the same equal liberty and equal distribution should be accepted in the new government with respect to the states. Ibid., 62.

23 Ibid., 69.

24 Ibid., 65.
25 Ibid., 70.
26 Ibid., 41 (Sherman), 44 (Lansing), 70 (Martin), 71 (Bedford).
27 See, e.g., ibid., 38 (Paterson).
28 E.g., ibid., 66–67, 69.
29 E.g., Reynolds v. Sims, 377 U.S. 573 (1964).
30 See *Notes of Debates in the Federal Convention of 1787 Reported by James Madison* (New York: W.W. Norton, 1966), 295.
31 See Benedict Anderson, *Imagined Communities* (London: Verso Books, rev. ed. 2016).
32 The state-egalitarians might plausibly have argued that Wilson and Madison and Hamilton intuitively understood all of this– or that they were estopped to dismiss political communities like states as "imaginary beings." They were after all determined to create a new "imaginary being"– the new nation of the United States of America– that would be no less "artificial" than the states of Virginia and North Carolina and the others. And it was they who conceived of "We the People of the United States" that could be brought into existence and then used to ratify the document.
33 For elaboration of the point, see Steven D. Smith, *Fictions, Lies, and the Authority of Law* (Notre Dame, Indiana: University of Notre Dame Press, 2021).
34 Larson and Winship, *The Constitutional Convention*, 62–63.
35 Ibid., 62.
36 Ibid., 72–74.
37 Ibid., 40.
38 Ibid., 68–69.
39 Ibid., 73.
40 Ibid.
41 Ibid., 74–78.
42 *Notes of Debates in the Federal Convention of 1787*, 289.
43 Larson and Winship, *The Constitutional Convention*, 291–92.
44 Ibid., 293–95.
45 Ibid., 294. Indeed, even before the committee returned with its compromise, Wilson had anticipated it, and had explained its incoherence. "If one branch . . . should be chosen by legislatures and the other by the people," he objected, "the two branches will rest on different foundations, and dissensions will naturally arise between them." Ibid., 34. If justice required proportionate representation in one branch, how could a departure from that principle be permitted in the other? "The rule of suffrage ought on every principle to be the same in the second as in the first branch." Ibid., 69.
46 *Notes of Debates in the Federal Convention of 1787*, 293.
47 Larson and Winship, *The Constitutional Convention*, 75.
48 Ibid., 7.
49 *Notes of Debates in the Federal Convention of 1787*, 297.
50 Ibid., 298–99.
51 Ibid., 301–02.
52 James Madison, "Federalist No. 39," in *The Federalist Papers*, 242.
53 Ellis, *The Quartet*, 170–72.

54 Madison, "Federalist No. 37" in *The Federalist Papers*, 226.
55 Ibid., 222, 226–27.
56 Larson and Winship, *The Constitutional Convention*, 90; see also ibid., 106 (Pinckney).
57 Larson and Winship, *The Constitutional Convention*, 131.
58 Ibid., 81.
59 Ibid., 87
60 Ibid., 112.
61 Ibid., 112–13.
62 Ibid., 111–12.
63 Ibid., 128.
64 Ibid., 130.
65 Ibid., 88, 129, 131.
66 Ibid., 133.
67 Ibid., 129.
68 Cf. Allen C. Guelzo, "How Slavery Is and Isn't in the Constitution," *Public Discourse*, November 8, 2018, https://www.thepublicdiscourse.com/2018/11/42658/.
69 See Ellis, *The Quartet*, 144 (observing that "slavery was deeply embedded in the economies of all states south of the Potomac and . . . no political plan that questioned that reality had any prospect of winning approval.").
70 Ibid., 145.
71 See Larson and Winship, *The Constitutional Convention*, 187.
72 Ellis, *The Quartet*, 151.

PART II

Four (Somewhat) Skeptical Perspectives

Chapter Two

The Not-Your-Ancestors' Principle-Plush Constitution

Steven D. Smith

In the previous chapter, we saw how the American framers, in order to avert imminent national disintegration, devised a legalistic Constitution that was cobbled together with compromises and utterly bereft of grand statements of principles or ideals (after its first sentence anyway). The framers fashioned this sort of principle-barren constitution not because they themselves lacked principles or vision, but rather because they *did* have a vision—of a unified America—and they understood that a more principled constitution would not have furthered, but rather would have defeated, their unifying purpose. Although by comparison to present-day demographics the population of that time may seem remarkably homogeneous to us, Founding-era Americans were nonetheless deeply divided on some fundamental questions of justice and political morality, including slavery. Any attempt to resolve those divisions in the new Constitution would merely have ensured that the document could not have been ratified.

And so the framers managed to "rise above principle" and construct a frame of governance that would hold the nation together for the next seven decades and then, following one catastrophic conflagration, for the next century and a half. We are living with and under that Constitution still.

Sort of.

If we just innocently read the words of what today is called "the Constitution," these seem to be identical to the words that emerged from the Philadelphia convention—supplemented, to be sure, by a handful of formally adopted amendments. But imagine that we are, say, historians from some distant future time, and that the actual text of the Constitution has somehow been lost, so that we have to try to extrapolate what the Constitution is, or was, from the ways in which it is used and referred to in contemporary constitutional scholarship and professional and popular discourse. We might infer that the document was something altogether different from the nuts-and-boltsy, compromise-ridden, rhetoric-and ideal-starved text that the framers scratched together. We might instead surmise that the Constitution was, as one prominent scholar put it, a "rich lode of principle."[1] Or that it was, as Justice William Brennan enthused, some kind of "sublime oration on the dignity of man."[2] That is the kind of Constitution that is invoked and presupposed in a good deal of professional and popular discourse today.

How did this transformation come about? The short answer is that modern jurists, scholars, politicians, advocates, and citizens—some of them anyway—have *wanted* and even *needed* the Constitution to be a repository of principles, or a sublime oration on human dignity, and so they have insisted on treating it as such,[3] the actual text of the document be damned. In this chapter we will survey how this transformation happened. And we will ask whether this is a transformation that we should celebrate or lament.

PRINCIPILIZING THE CONSTITUTION

We cannot—and, fortunately, for present purposes we need not—attempt any comprehensive history of how the Constitution came to be transformed in the professional and popular understanding from a workmanlike legal document into a repository of majestic principles. It will be enough to observe the modern trajectory of this development by looking at influential expositions by three leading legal scholars from three successive generations: Herbert Wechsler, Ronald Dworkin, and Jack Balkin.

This focus on legal scholars may prompt a question that hovers around any venture in intellectual history: do the articulations of thinkers or academic theorists act as *causal influences* with respect to historical developments? Or are such theoretical productions rather *expressions* or *distillations* of ideas that are somehow "in the air," or that other people of the period also intuit and embrace (perhaps in more inchoate or less fancy form)? Does the philosophizing of a Dewey, say, or a Rawls, or a Dworkin, move thought and even politics and culture along particular channels? Or do these thinkers merely manage to present in more explicit and systematic form ideas and values and attitudes that are already sludging their way through those channels?

Probably the best and safest answer to that question would be: "A bit of both, in proportions that vary from thinker to thinker and from period to period."[4] There is, as Charles Taylor says, a "continuing flow between the thinker and his culture."[5] But in any case, though the question may arise, there is no need to answer it here. Whether Wechsler, Dworkin, and Balkin and their academic kin have shaped thinking about the Constitution or merely articulated common or fashionable tendencies of thought, their writings can serve to reflect the way in which the Constitution has been transformed from a primarily legal instrument into a repository of grand principles.

Herbert Wechsler's Neutral Principles

Herbert Wechsler, the Harlan Fiske Stone Professor at Columbia Law School and Director of the American Law Institute, was a giant of the profession and arguably the most prominent legal scholar of his generation; and in 1959 he was invited to give the most prestigious lecture in American legal academia: Harvard Law School's Oliver Wendell Holmes Lecture.[6] In its published form, the lecture would become the fifth-most- cited law review article in American history.[7] Read today after more than threescore years of furious constitutional activity and theorizing, the lecture can come across as intellectually bland, and also pompously quaint.[8] In its historical context, though, Wechsler's lecture was a portentous statement—even though, or perhaps because, it was in some significant respects substantially vacuous.

The lecture was important in part because of who gave it, in part because of when it was given, but most importantly because it anticipated or reflected a way of thinking about the Constitution that has come to be almost axiomatic in the legal profession. We have already noted Wechsler's eminence as a legal scholar. We can also appreciate in retrospect that 1959 stood at a crucial juncture in constitutional history. The Supreme Court's monumental decision in *Brown v. Board of Education*,[9] condemning racially segregated public schools and by implication official racial segregation in general, was just a half-decade old. *Brown* was on its way to becoming the indispensable decision in the modern American constitutional tradition. In respectable quarters the correctness of the decision has come to be regarded as beyond question; and yet the justification for the decision has proven controversial, and elusive (as Wechsler noted in his lecture). The ongoing enterprise of justifying *Brown* thus summoned up an outpouring of scholarly and professional creativity, which in turn has had the effect of legitimating a good deal more than *Brown* itself, which in turn has stimulated even further creativity. Thus, 1959 was situated on the brink of a period during which the Supreme Court, with the eager assistance of cadres of scholarly supporters, rationalizers, and apologists, would assume an increasingly prominent role in American governance—a role that has supervised the transformation of American law (and, by extension, of American politics and culture) in a whole variety of fields.

Wechsler, in short, was an important figure delivering an important lecture at a pivotal moment in American constitutional history. It is thus not surprising that his Holmes Lecture was portentous, foreshadowing a great deal of what would follow.

The main theme of the lecture was suggested in its title: "Toward Neutral Principles of Constitutional Law." After warming to his subject and strutting his intellectual agility by purporting to demonstrate that the power of judicial review (meaning the examination and potential invalidation by courts of legislative or executive actions) could be derived in somewhat roundabout and scholastic fashion from the text of the Constitution, Wechsler launched into that theme. His central claim was that in deciding whether laws or executive actions are constitutionally valid, courts are obligated to use reason rather than fiat, and to reason on the basis of "principles." It is this commitment to "principle," Wechsler argued, that distinguishes courts from legislatures or executive officials, and that prevents the Supreme Court itself from degenerating into a "naked power organ."[10]

There was nothing especially novel (as Wechsler acknowledged[11]) in the suggestion that judicial decisions should be based on reasoning. At least as long as we can remember, haven't courts always felt obligated to offer reasons for their decisions? Wechsler's contribution, it seems, in his own estimation and in that of his contemporaries, was to insist that judicial reasoning needed to be "principled"; and this was the idea that his lecture came to be remembered for, and repeatedly cited for.

The point may seem simple enough, and also quite commonsensical, but it is also surprisingly elusive. What does it mean, exactly, for reasoning to be "principled"? And what is the relation of "principled" judicial *reasoning* to *the Constitution* itself—to the actual document? With respect to the first of these questions, Wechsler said a good deal—though nothing that upon examination seems especially illuminating. With respect to the second question, Wechsler's answer anticipated an approach that has come to seem almost automatic to constitutionalists: in order for constitutional reasoning to be "principled," we must insist on viewing the constitutional text itself as, fundamentally, a repository of "principles."

Thus, Wechsler sought to explain both what principled reasoning *is* and what it *is not*; but upon reflection there is less in his explanations than meets the eye on first look. Constitutional adjudication, Wechsler argued, "must be genuinely principled, *resting on analysis and reasons quite transcending the immediate result* that is achieved."[12] That is what principled reasoning *is*—reasoning based on premises or considerations that extend beyond the case itself. The intended contrast is with what is sometimes called "result-oriented jurisprudence." Wechsler described this disfavored practice as "*ad hoc* evaluation," or as "judgment [that] turns on the immediate result."[13] And he gave examples: if a judge or critic approves or disapproves of a particular decision just because it involves "a claim put forward by a labor union or a taxpayer, a

Negro or a segregationist, a corporation or a Communist,"[14] then that judge or critic is engaged not in "principled" jurisprudence, but rather in its antithesis. Wechsler worried that this kind of *"ad hoc* evaluation" had become lamentably common; it was "the deepest problem of our constitutionalism."[15]

There is nothing extravagant in the suspicion that some or many of our Justices have engaged in politicized or "result-oriented" adjudication in some or many cases. The accusation is perfectly familiar, and far from implausible. Still, Wechsler's diagnosis of this practice in terms of "principled" adjudication versus *"ad hoc* evaluation" seems, upon examination, profoundly unhelpful.

Let us take his own explanation, and try to apply it: a "principled" decision is one that "rest[s] on analysis and reasons quite transcending the immediate result that is achieved."[16] That sounds right. And yet, if we think about it . . . , well, don't *all* judicial decisions do that, or at least purport to do that? Judicial decisions of any consequence always give reasons for the results they reach, and those reasons inevitably refer to considerations or premises that go beyond, or "transcend," the immediate result to be achieved in the particular case. If they did not, how could we recognize them as "reasons" at all? After all, to say that a decision is compelled by a rule or standard, or to say that the decision is "just" or "fair" or supported by sound public policy, is already to appeal to considerations that go beyond the particular case.

Indeed, what would a decision that did not offer reasons transcending the particular result even look like? "Jones wins because . . . he is Jones"? This would be a shabby opinion, no doubt; but the fact is that courts simply do not offer decisions that look or sound like this. And even if they did, it is still not clear that Wechsler's analysis would identify what the deficiency is. A decision declaring that "Jones wins because he is Jones" would imply a more general premise transcending the particular case—that in controversies involving people named Jones (or maybe *this particular* Jones?), Jones should win. Though exceedingly fortunate for Jones, that is no doubt an absurd premise for a legal decision. But its absurdity does not consist of any failure to transcend the particular case; on the contrary, the premise does in fact extend well beyond the case, or the "immediate result."

For similar reasons, Wechsler's counterexamples of unprincipled decisions—cases in which a party wins because it or he is "a labor union or a taxpayer, a Negro or a segregationist, a corporation or a Communist"—fail to support his point. Consider an extreme hypothetical instance. Suppose that Judge Engels is a dyed-in-the-wool Communist; and regardless of the specific facts, and regardless of whether the case is one in contract or tort or criminal law, Judge Engels always rules in favor of parties who happen to be Communists. Such a practice may be an egregious violation of the judge's duties—but *not* because the judge's decisions are not based on reasons that transcend the particular case. On the contrary, each decision is entirely based on a premise that transcends the particular case: Communists win.

Wechsler or a supporter might respond that a proposition like "Communists win" or "labor unions win," while admittedly a general *proposition* or premise, is not a *"principle."* And perhaps it isn't: in order to qualify as a "principle," perhaps, a proposition has to have some sort of *moral* content or to pass some moral or ontological test. But if so, Wechsler made no attempt to explain what that moral or ontological test might be or, more fundamentally, how general propositions that are not "principles" are to be distinguished from general propositions that *are* "principles." He did emphasize, to be sure, that the judge's reasons need to be "neutral." But this evidently did not mean that the reasons must be "value free," or something of that sort, because Wechsler admitted that all legal judgments involve assessments of and choices among values.[17]

In context, the requirement of "neutrality" seems merely to mean that the court or the judge should apply reasons or principles consistently in the various cases in which they are implicated: a judge should not apply a particular consideration in one case and then ignore it in the next. But on that understanding, it is still not clear why Judge Engels, who consistently acts on the premise "Communists win," and so always rules in favor of Communists, is not acting in an admirably and indeed consummately principled way.

This difficulty anticipates a problem that sweepingly afflicts modern constitutional jurisprudence: jurists and scholars routinely insist that constitutional adjudication must be "principled," or that the Constitution is a "repository of principles," but it can be maddeningly difficult to try to figure out just what a "principle" is.[18] We will consider this problem more closely in chapter 3. For now, though, let us bracket this difficulty and proceed to consider an even more portentous aspect of Wechsler's lecture. Wechsler's subject was constitutional adjudication—or adjudication of cases under the Constitution—but at least for the first few portions of his discussion, his focus was not on *what the Constitution is*, or on how the Constitution works or means, but rather on *courts*: how should courts behave? It is almost as if, in discoursing about how adjudication must be "principled," Wechsler had lost interest in the question of the relation of constitutional adjudication to that venerable text we call "the Constitution." But then, as if suddenly noticing this potentially embarrassing oversight, Wechsler returned to discuss the connection of "principled" adjudication to the actual Constitution. And what he said again foreshadowed an approach that has become almost axiomatic in much constitutional discourse.

Thus, midway through the lecture, Wechsler clarified that constitutional decisions, in addition to being "principled," should also be faithful to constitutional text, history, and precedent. Or at least he implied as much.[19] Sort of.

Actually, Wechsler did not exactly and forthrightly assert that courts must be faithful to constitutional text and history. His approach was more subtle, or perhaps more evasive: he protested that he should not be taken as *denying* that claim. Thus, Wechsler said that although his emphasis had been on "principled" reasoning, this emphasis should not be taken "to imply that I depreciate the duty of fidelity to the text of the Constitution."[20] Same for history and precedent: without positively *affirming* much less explaining the authority of these factors, he cautioned that he should not be understood as *denying* their importance.[21]

But these backhanded acknowledgments were immediately subjected to summary but seemingly debilitating qualifications that reduced or removed any constraining force these conventional legal features might have. Start with history. Wechsler acknowledged that history "has weight." But what does it mean for history to have "weight," and how does that "weight" exert itself? Having acknowledged history's weight, Wechsler hastened to caution that "it is surely subtle business to appraise [history] as a guide."[22] Nor did Wechsler say anything more about how that "subtle business" should be performed.

Perhaps through the conventional invoking and distinguishing of legal precedents? That is what lawyers and judges have typically done. And indeed Wechsler acknowledged that precedents need to be taken into account. And yet . . . the authority of a precedent "'depend[s] altogether on the force of the reasoning by which it is supported.'"[23] Which implies that a precedent should be followed just to the extent that it coincides with what "principled" reasoning would prescribe anyway—which in turn implies that the precedent itself contributes nothing of substance to the outcome.

And what about that seeming bedrock of legal authorities—the constitutional text itself? While acknowledging (or at least insisting that he should not be taken as denying) the "duty of fidelity" to text, Wechsler promptly added two vitiating qualifications. First, a text should be understood in terms of the value or principle of which it is a manifestation. He quoted Chief Justice Charles Evans Hughes: "'Behind the words of the constitutional provisions are postulates which limit and control.'"[24] Second, the duty of fidelity to text applies "when its [the text's] words may be decisive."[25] In other words, if a constitutional text clearly commands a particular result, then the courts are obligated to follow that text. But in litigated cases that reach the Supreme Court, how often does that condition obtain?

Rarely, it seems, at least in Wechsler's view. Thus, Wechsler noted the familiar distinction which holds that some constitutional texts, like the due process clause, are cast in sweeping and thus principle-friendly terms, while other provisions seem to have a more concrete and thus constraining meaning. It is a common enough distinction, and we will see it again—and again, and again. Anticipating a later generation of creative deconstructionists,[26] though, Wechsler challenged the distinction. Even the Constitution's seemingly specific provisions, he argued, *can be* read to be more open and uncertain—and thus more "principled"—than they appear to be.[27] Conversely, even provisions which today may seem vague and general may once have had a fairly definite and confined meaning, when they were initially adopted; but the important point is that they need not be read *now* in accordance with that historical meaning. Rather, they *can be* read as expressing principles that are susceptible to a broader—much broader—interpretation.

As an example, Wechsler acknowledged that the Fourteenth Amendment's due process and equal protection clauses *could* be read in fairly narrow and concrete terms, and that those clauses might actually have been so understood at the time of their enactment. But "I cannot find it in my heart to regret that interpretation did not ground itself in ancient history but rather has perceived in these provisions a compendious affirmation of the basic values of a free society."[28]

Nor should this manner of interpretation be limited to the due process and equal protection clauses. Thus, Wechsler added that "we should prefer to see the other clauses of the Bill of Rights read as an affirmation of the special values they embody rather than as statements of a finite rule of law."[29] Maybe so, although at this point the counsel seems almost superfluous. Seriously: once the clauses of the Fourteenth Amendment have been liberated from their initially concrete meanings to become instead "a compendious affirmation of the basic values of a free society," what more does the expansive constitutionalist really need?

And the justification for this vastly inflationary reading, once again, was that "we should prefer it," or that Wechlser himself *liked it* (or could not "find it in [his] heart to regret it"). He *wanted* to have a constitution of principles, and he insisted on viewing the actual Constitution as the kind of thing he wanted.

Or perhaps this description underestimates Wechsler's rationale. A more dignified description might go like this: 1) Judicial review, in order to be legitimate, must be "principled." 2) But judicial review must also be grounded in, or at least cannot be detached from, the actual Constitution, or the constitutional text. 3) In order for judicial review to be both "principled" and grounded in the constitutional text, that text needs to be viewed as a source of principles, not merely of "finite rule[s] of law." 4) We should therefore prefer (or not "find it in our hearts to regret") interpretations that insist on viewing constitutional provisions as expressions of general values or principles rather than as finite rules of law—whether or not that is what their enactors intended or what their words would have been understood to mean at the time of enactment.

There is much in this reasoning that might be questioned. For present purposes, though, the important point is that Wechsler's approach to the Constitution would come to be almost axiomatic to, and would be expanded on by, future generations of constitutionalists.

Ronald Dworkin's "Moral Reading" of the Constitution.

Professor Wechsler's lecture was concerned with the legitimacy of *judicial review*. A generation later, Professor Ronald Dworkin, of Yale, Oxford, and NYU, greatly expanded this concern: Dworkin sought a jurisprudential account that would justify the legitimacy of *law generally*, and indeed of the government from which law issues. Perhaps the most prominent and influential legal theorist of his time, Dworkin built on some of the same themes that Wechsler had treated, but he did so at much greater length and with much greater philosophical sophistication; he was, we might say, Wechsler on philosophical steroids. And his efforts yielded a Constitution that was even more overtly conceived of as a repository of grand moral principles and ideals.

A theory of law, Dworkin argued, should have as its purpose "a justification for the use of collective power against individual citizens and groups,"[30] or a justification for "the moral authority of law."[31] In other words, legal theory was directed to "the classical problem of the legitimacy of coercive power."[32] In this respect, Dworkin was addressing the same problem that James Wilson and James Madison were concerned with when they argued for proportional representation at the Philadelphia convention. Unlike Wilson and Madison and Jefferson, however, Dworkin found the classic American answer—namely, that legitimacy must be based on "the consent of the governed"—to be wholly unsatisfactory. That idea, along with the related notion of a "social contract," might work "if every citizen were party to an actual, historical agreement to obey political decisions taken in the way his community's political decisions are in fact taken."[33] But of course there has been no such agreement: the notion is a "fantasy."[34] Nor do other common accounts of authority—accounts based on a supposed "duty to be just" or on notions of "fair play"—do any better.[35]

So then how *is* authority to be justified? Dworkin developed an elaborate account of "associative obligations" that apply to us by virtue of our being part of a community, whether or not we consent to join that community.[36] And yet not just any community can generate such obligations. Rather, it is only a special kind of community—what Dworkin called a "community of principle"—that can support obligation and hence authority. "A community of principle ... can claim the authority of a genuine associative community and can therefore claim moral legitimacy—that its collective decisions are matters of obligation and not bare power."³⁷ Where Wechsler turned to principles to prevent *the Supreme Court* from being a "naked power organ," Dworkin invoked principles to prevent *the law generally* and the political community from being exercises of "bare power."

In order to qualify as a "community of principle," however, a community and its law must meet stringent requirements. More specifically, government in such a community should "act on a single, coherent set of principles even when its citizens are divided about what the right principles of justice and fairness really are."³⁸ The citizens must "accept that their fates are linked in the following strong way: they accept that they are governed by common principles, not just by rules hammered out in political compromise."³⁹ These common principles must be understood as the product of a community imagined in a particular way. More specifically, Dworkin insisted that judges must "identify legal rights and duties, so far as possible, on the assumption that they were all created by a single author—the community personified—expressing a coherent conception of justice and fairness."⁴⁰

In reality, of course, American community does *not* consist—and never has consisted—of a single author expressing a single coherent conception of fairness and justice. Not even close. On the contrary, right from the outset, America has consisted of a vast, diverse, often contentious multitude acting on very different conceptions of justice and fairness. Having rejected the founders' idea that legitimacy is based on the consent of the governed as a "fantasy," it seems that Dworkin was making legitimacy dependent on an even more extravagant fantasy.

This account of legitimacy in law seems eminently contestable, and we will return to consider it in due course. For now, though, we need to appreciate how Dworkin's account of legal legitimacy dictated for him how the Constitution must be understood. Simply put: in order to be authoritative or legitimate, the Constitution *must be* viewed as a manifestation of a coherent set of principles—*not* as a product of political compromises, and not as a merely legal instrument with (and here the contempt is almost palpable) "the texture and tone of an insurance policy or a standard form of commercial lease."⁴¹ So Dworkin advocated a "moral reading" that "proposes that we all—judges, lawyers, citizens—interpret and apply [the Constitution's] abstract clauses on the understanding that they invoke moral principles about political decency and justice."⁴²

And so Dworkin proceeded to reconceive the Constitution in these terms. Thus, in Dworkin's "moral reading," the First Amendment "recognizes a moral principle."⁴³ Likewise the Fifth Amendment, and the Fourteenth: all of these "must be understood . . . [to] refer to abstract moral principles" which should be understood "at the most general possible level."⁴⁴ In particular, the

Fourteenth Amendment's equal protection clause "declared a principle of breathtaking scope and power."⁴⁵

Dworkin knew, of course, that merely as a matter of mundane historical fact (as we saw in the previous chapter), political compromises—which he denounced—have shaped the making of the Constitution. He also acknowledged that the document contains provisions—such as the Third Amendment, prohibiting quartering of soldiers—that would be difficult to read as expressing any kind of general principle.⁴⁶ But in his overall presentation, these grudging concessions seemed to reflect a sort of "confession and avoidance strategy": the more "legal" and less "principled" constitutional provisions are acknowledged—and then quickly retired from view in favor of the more apparently abstract and thus "principled" provisions.

Thus, Dworkin at one point acknowledged that the provisions of the Bill of Rights vary significantly in their levels of abstraction: not all of them are worded in terms suggestive of any "principle."⁴⁷ But a few pages later the qualification seemed to have been forgotten: "The Bill of Rights, as I said, consists of broad and abstract principles of political morality, which together encompass, in exceptionally abstract form, all the dimensions of political morality that in our political culture can ground an individual constitutional right."⁴⁸ It is "not a list of discrete remedies . . . , but a commitment to an ideal of just government."⁴⁹

In much the same way, the more seemingly abstract and hence "principled" provisions are projected onto—and are taken as determining the character of—the Constitution as a whole. The upshot is an exhilarating "vision of the Constitution as a system of principle."⁵⁰ "The Constitution is America's moral sail, and we must hold to the courage of the conviction that fills it, the conviction that we can all be equal citizens of a moral republic. That is a noble faith, and only optimism can redeem it."⁵¹

Jack Balkin's Redemption Story.

These same themes and terms—principle, faith, and in particular redemption—animate the constitutional theorizing of Jack Balkin, currently the Knight Professor of Constitutional Law and the First Amendment at Yale Law School and one of the most prominent and prolific contemporary scholars of constitutional law. Balkin's view of the Constitution is similar to Dworkin's in some important respects and dissimilar in other important respects. But in perceiving the Constitution as in its essence a statement of lofty principles, Balkin concurs with Dworkin (and with most other modern scholars and jurists).

Like Dworkin, Balkin is concerned with the problem of "legitimacy."⁵² But Balkin has a distinctive emphasis: he seeks an account for "understanding and explaining legitimate *change*."⁵³ American government today plainly works very differently than it did a century ago, and a century ago it worked differently than it did a century before that. Enthusiastically progressive in his political and jurisprudential commitments, Balkin rejoices in such change. Even so, he wonders what it is that can render such change "legitimate"?

Balkin's answer begins by emphasizing—or at least appearing to emphasize—the fundamental force of the constitutional *text*. It is only the text, he says, that is constant enough to connect successive generations of Americans and concrete enough to enlist the allegiance of ordinary citizens.⁵⁴

On first reflection, one might suppose that his emphasis on text would distinguish Balkin from someone like Dworkin, for whom (as we have seen) legitimacy is fundamentally linked to a "coherent set of principles," and it might also seem to commit Balkin to a static and conservative constitutional jurisprudence. But these suppositions would be mistaken. Having insisted on the primacy of text, Balkin promptly casts off any constraints that might be associated with that commitment by describing the constitutional text as a manifestation of lofty principles that can stretch and expand as the times require.

Thus, like Dworkin, and like Wechsler before him, Balkin repeatedly claims that the Constitution "features general and abstract concepts," uses "the vague and abstract language of principles," and embodies principles that are "broad, abstract, or vague."⁵⁵ It is for Americans "a source of important values, including justice, equality, democracy, and human rights" which are "objects of aspiration."⁵⁶ The Constitution "serves as a kind of higher law—it states ideals of liberty, equality, and democracy that people seek to live up to over time."⁵⁷

Actually, like Dworkin, Balkin admits that not *everything* in the Constitution speaks in "the language of principles." Some provisions contain "rules," others adopt "standards," and still others manifest "principles."⁵⁸ But again as with Dworkin, it is the provisions containing principles that for Balkin seem to give the Constitution its essential character. Thus, he often describes his approach to constitutional interpretation as "the method of text and principle."⁵⁹ *Not* as the "method of text and *rule,* with the occasional standard or principle."

Or, instead of "principles," Balkin often likes to talk of "promises."⁶⁰ The founders made "promises" to themselves and their posterity—promises of justice and equality. (Or, conflating and consolidating the generations, Balkin talks of "the people" making "promises to themselves."⁶¹) Aware that the text of the original Constitution contains very little that looks like "promises," Balkin turns instead to the Declaration of Independence, with its language of "unalienable rights" and of all people being "created equal."⁶² These lofty promises could not be and hence were not immediately fulfilled, and so it has fallen to subsequent generations to interpret and progressively honor them—to "redeem" the Constitution's promises. Ultimately, it is the peoples' faith in this project of redemption that gives legitimacy to the Constitution and to constitutional change.

Again in seeming contrast to Dworkin, who emphasizes the primacy of judges and even more so philosophers in interpreting the Constitution's meaning,[63] Balkin argues in more democratic tones that "the people" should have priority. The Constitution is a document not for elites but for "the people."[64] Or at least this is what Balkin *says*, again and again. But unlike the "popular constitutionalism" favored by former Stanford law dean Larry Kramer,[65] Balkin's ostensible insistence on the primacy of "the people" does not lead him to diminish in any way the power of elites—of judges—forcibly to impose their own understandings on "the people."

In fact, his "method of text and principle" in practice appears to enhance judges' power in this respect. Thus, unlike other progressive constitutionalists who even in supporting liberal constitutional decisions about matters such as abortion and homosexual rights have worried about whether and how these decisions can be justified under the Constitution,[66] Balkin appears to be serenely untroubled: once the principled nature of the Constitution is understood, he suggests, such decisions are easy to justify, and indeed are overdetermined.[67] Thus, Balkin sees no need to say which provision in the Constitution the rights of abortion or LGBT rights are based on. Once the Constitution's provisions are dissolved into the "principles" or "promises" of which they are supposedly manifestations, the question loses its interest: any number of constitutional provisions can do the job, and you can pick whichever provision you happen to prefer.[68]

Such decisions, of course, work by invalidating laws adopted by legislatures supposedly chosen by and representing "the people." In Balkin's democratically toned account, it seems, "the people" whose democratic decisions are thus overruled, or who are sanctioned for not respecting the judges' interpretations, are evidently to be consoled by the assurance that they still have the right to protest that the judges got things wrong—and to believe that at some future time, or perhaps on some ethereal redemptive plane, if not on the level of mundane practice, it is still "the people's" interpretations that are entitled to priority.

The Triumph of Principle

We have seen how three prominent constitutional scholars in three successive generations have embraced the notion of the Constitution not so much as a legal document but rather as a repository of lofty moral and political principles, such as "justice" and "equality," to be interpreted and enforced by judges. All three of these scholars were or are liberal or progressive in their political orientations, and that fact might lead one to infer that the "principled" Constitution is basically a liberal or progressive notion. But the inference would be mistaken. It may be true that liberals like Dworkin or (on the bench) Justice William Brennan have been more enthusiastic about the vision of the Constitution as principled—principled in a "living" way—than conservative scholars or Justices (like Antonin Scalia) have been. Even so, while disagreeing about the content or generality of the Constitution's principles, both liberals and conservatives have generally accepted this picture of the Constitution as an embodiment of fundamental principles. And there are understandable reasons for this development.

For one, conservatives as much as liberals have wanted to affirm some constitutional decisions that are difficult to justify just in terms of the Constitution's text or the expectations of the people who enacted its relevant provisions. Probably the best known instance is *Brown v. Board of Education*.[69] Most conservative scholars and Justices in recent decades have insisted on their support for *Brown*; to do otherwise would risk excommunication from the community of respectable constitutionalists. But it is generally accepted that the Americans who drafted and enacted the Fourteenth Amendment did not believe that the provision would require desegregation of public schools.[70] This fact has challenged conservatives to devise rationales for affirming *Brown*. And perhaps the most common rationale—one exemplified in the work of the conspicuously conservative, failed Supreme Court nominee Robert Bork—explains that the Fourteenth Amendment adopted a "principle of equality"; and whatever its enactors' expectations may have been, we now know that this principle is incompatible with racially segregated schools.[71]

This specific point leads to a more general one. Conservative jurists and scholars have tended to favor an approach in which the Constitution would be interpreted and enforced according to its "original meaning," and they have criticized the notion of a "living Constitution." And yet it has also seemed to most of them that "original meaning" cannot be confined to a provision's "original expected applications." It is not just that such a confined understanding would lead to regrettable results (as in *Brown*). Insistence on "original expected applications" would have the unacceptable consequence—or so it might seem—of rendering the Constitution irrelevant to a host of modern issues that the enactors could not have anticipated and about which they therefore had no expectations.

To take a familiar example: acting in 1789, the framers of the Fourth Amendment regulation of searches and seizures presumably had no specific expectations about the possible immunity of telephone communications from intrusive and unauthorized wiretaps.[72] Or we might push the worry to an absurd extreme: if the meaning of a constitutional provision is equated with its "expected applications," then under a radically nominalistic conception, the term "persons" as used in various places in the Constitution, would extend to those individual human beings that the enactors had in mind. Would it thus cease to have any effect once the framers' generation had passed out of existence? The conclusion seems absurd, to be sure, but how exactly is it to be avoided.

Such concerns inform the almost universal rejection—including by self-styled "originalists" and conservatives—of "expected applications" as the touchstone of "original meaning." But if a constitutional provision's meaning is not given by what its enactors expected of it, then what *does* provide that meaning? A convenient and comfortable solution has been to understand a provision's "meaning" in terms of the "principle" that it ostensibly embodies and reflects. Since a "principle" presumably transcends and continues to exist after the generation that endorsed it has passed away, the problem of temporal limitations on the application of the Constitution is thereby solved. The Fourth Amendment covers wiretaps, even if its authors never contemplated the possibility of wiretaps, because the provision embodies something like a "principle of privacy" that extends to any sort of governmental intrusion.

Thus, conservatives and liberals alike have gravitated toward viewing constitutional meanings in terms of "principles." This move renders largely otiose the long-standing debates between proponents of "original meaning" and the "living Constitution," as Professor Balkin has noticed in arguing for what he calls "living originalism." Although the old debates persist, it increasingly seems that what actually divides conservatives from liberals is merely disagreements over *which* principles should be extracted from the Constitution, or *how broadly* those principles should be stated, or what the *practical entailments* of those principles are. All sides seem to have converged in regarding the Constitution as a statement of "principles" of some kind.

Whether this move to "principles" is as necessary for originalists as is sometimes supposed is no doubt debatable.[73] The extreme nominalism that would understand my use of the word "persons" to refer only to the particular Toms, Dicks, and Harrys that I happen to have in mind as I utter the word is surely not mandatory, to put the point charitably. Rather, we can and normally do understand the word to refer to a general category—a category, obviously, of human beings—that encompasses any number of individuals whom I never met or imagined. Nor is there any compelling reason why *general classes* or categories must be understood in terms of normative or moral "principles." We routinely use categories of varying degrees of generality—apples or, more generally, fruits or, more generally, food or, more generally, material objects—without reducing these categories to the specific instances we might have in mind—but also without imagining that the categories must refer to some sort of "principles." In similar fashion, without reducing constitutional provisions to their "expected applications," the terms of the Fourth Amendment ("searches and seizures"), or the Seventh Amendment ("suits at common law," "right of trial by jury"), or even the Fourteenth Amendment ("due process of law," "equal protection of the laws"), might be understood to describe general classes or concepts but not to be affirmations of implicit "moral principles." Much less, to borrow from Dworkin, of moral "principles that are breathtaking in their scope."

Still, whether or not it was necessary or inevitable, the move to treat "principles" as the content or ingredient of "meaning" has been common, even among conservatives. The understanding of the Constitution as a manifestation or embodiment of "principles" has become close to axiomatic. And so we might ask: is this transformation of our Constitution from a workmanlike legal instrument—a sort of nuts-and-boltsy framework of government—into a repository of principles something that we should celebrate? Or that we should regret?

Constitutional Principles and Legal Legitimacy

As we have seen, the influential constitutional thinkers we have considered—Herbert Wechsler, Ronald Dworkin, and Jack Balkin—all connected the principled Constitution to the need for "legitimacy." Wechsler was concerned with the legitimacy of *judicial review*, Dworkin with the legitimacy of *law* and government generally, and Balkin with the legitimacy of constitutional *change*. Each of these scholars contended that the legitimacy they—and we—need is possible only under a Constitution understood as a body of principles. If they were right, then we may be grateful for the transformation of the Constitution into such a document, because otherwise we would be living under an illegitimate legal regime. And who wants that?

But *were* these scholars right in linking legitimacy to a principled Constitution? In this respect, it was Dworkin who offered the most carefully worked out account. So we should consider his account more closely.

As we have noted, Dworkin explicitly rejected the standard American account of governmental and legal legitimacy—namely, the account that holds that government and law must be based on "the consent of the governed." This proposition was of course declared to be a self-evident truth in the Declaration of Independence, and it has dominated American thinking ever since. Alexander Meiklejohn asserted that "governments, we insist, derive their just powers from the consent of the governed. If that consent be lacking, governments have no just powers."[74] Rogers Smith explained that a feature of "the course of America's constitutional development" has been an "expanding legal emphasis on consent as the *sole* source of political legitimacy."[75] Dworkin nonetheless rejected the "consent of the governed" account because, he argued, Americans have never in fact given such consent. So the ostensible consent is a fiction or, as he put it, a "fantasy."[76] And he proposed his associative theory in which legitimacy and authority arise within a "community of principle" as a superior alternative.

In describing the consent account as a fiction, Dworkin surely had a point. There never has been an occasion, historically or today, in which all Americans have been given a meaningful opportunity to consent to the regime that governs us or, conversely, to withhold such consent. Even so, it has been argued elsewhere that a fiction can be a basis of political and legal authority—of legitimacy—on two conditions. First, the fiction needs to be, if not precisely true, at least plausible or "truish." Second, the fiction needs to provide some benefit or payoff to those who embrace or indulge the fiction.[77]

And in fact we are all perfectly familiar with using fictions in this way. So we go to a movie, and sit in rapt attention for two hours watching a series of enacted events while bracketing or suspending our awareness that these event never actually happened. We are willing and able to do this—to play along with the fiction—provided that the story is at least plausible, or "truish," and also that the story is entertaining or uplifting or insightful. Conversely, the fiction can fail in either of two basic ways. It will fail if it is too clumsy or implausible, so that we simply cannot manage to suspend our disbelief. Or the fiction will fail if it provides no payoff in terms of entertainment or edification, so that we have no incentive to bracket our awareness that the story "isn't really true."

In a similar way, political fictions can ground authority or legitimacy if they meet the necessary conditions. Once again, a viable political fiction does not need to be *true*, exactly, but it does need to be plausible or truish. And it needs to provide the benefits of valuable governance—social order, coordination, cooperation for the common good.[78]

In these terms, the "consent of the governed" account has arguably performed relatively well over the decades. It is surely true, as Dworkin says, that not every American in the founding period actually consented to the new Constitution, nor have Americans since then been afforded a realistic choice to consent or not consent. And yet the founders went to considerable effort to make the consent of the governed as plausible or truish as possible—by submitting the Constitution to widespread public debate and then to popular conventions in every state.[79] To be sure, not all Americans chose to—or indeed were permitted to—participate in this ratification process; even so, there was a plausible sense in which "We the People" could be said to have ratified the document. And the government has since that time been supported by broadening efforts and measures—including a vast expansion of the franchise and a more aggressive protection of freedom of speech—calculated to permit people to participate in the process of governance. Such opportunities to participate may not amount to actual "consent" to be governed, but they make the fiction of such consent seem plausible, or truish.

In this respect, contrast the standard "consent of the governed" account with Dworkin's alternative theory, in which, once again, citizens "accept that their fates are linked in the following strong way: they accept that they are governed by common principles, not just by rules hammered out in political compromise."[80] The citizens embrace "the assumption that [their legal rights and duties] were all created by a single author—the community personified—expressing a coherent conception of justice and fairness."[81] How plausible is *that* assumption—the assumption on which, in Dworkin's theory, the legitimacy of our law depends?

The unnuanced answer would be . . . not plausible at all. Not even remotely plausible.

Thus, with respect to the founding, Dworkin's assumption is simply and manifestly false. As we saw in the previous chapter, the Constitution was not the product of commonly held principles; on the contrary, the document consisted of rules and provisions "hammered out in political compromise," as Dworkin puts it.

The same can be said of other major amendments. For example, the transformative Reconstruction Amendments were not only the product of compromise, but were ratified only through massive coercion of the southern states, as scholars like Bruce Ackerman have shown.[82] And modern constitutional decisions on major issues—abortion, capital punishment, corporate free speech rights, same-sex marriage—have surely not been the product of any mutually shared "coherent conception of justice and fairness." Anyone who naively supposed as much would be promptly disabused of the pleasant illusion by reading the vociferous dissenting opinions in cases like *Obergefell*, *Citizens United*, or *Casey*.

It seems ironic that Dworkin would dismiss the "consent of the governed" account as a "fantasy" and then propose a replacement that openly trades on a blatant and transparent fiction—the idea of our law as the product of "a single author—the community personified"—and that depends on a description of our constitutional tradition that comes across as some sort of fantastic romantic hallucination. Though both the standard "consent of the governed" account and Dworkin's "community of principle" account may rest on fictions, just in terms of plausibility or truishness, the standard account is unquestionably the stronger candidate.

But perhaps Dworkin's account makes up for this plausibility deficit in terms of the other requirement—payoff, or benefit? Dworkin suggested that "consent" was incapable of supplying legitimacy to law, whereas his "community of principle" account *could* deliver that much needed payoff. But once again, that claim seems manifestly untenable.

To see how, let us for the moment treat each account's central fiction as if it were fact. Start with the consent account. If all of us did in fact consent to our legal regime, then it *would* seem plausible—wouldn't it?—to say that the laws adopted by that regime wield legitimate authority over us.

But now let us imagine that although we have not consented to our governmental regime, all of the laws adopted and promulgated by that regime are the product of a single author acting under a coherent theory of justice. Why would that fact create any sense of obligation on the part of those of us who do not agree with that single dominant theory? Suppose the government is attempting to coerce your obedience to some law that you are resisting because you regard the law as deeply unjust; and then someone explains that the law, along with all our other laws, is actually the product of a single author acting on the basis of a single coherent (although in your view deeply mistaken) conception of justice. Let us suppose that this explanation is plausible: what will your reaction be? "Well, in that case, I guess I'm obligated after all"? Or "so what?"

The second reaction seems more probable, and more plausible. If you think the law is unjust, why should it matter to you that the law comes from a single author acting under a coherent (albeit, in your view, misguided) conception of justice?

If anything, the "single author" account should make your situation seem even more oppressive. Put it this way: if you understand your legal system to be the product of trade-offs and compromises, then you will likely agree with some of the resulting laws and disagree with others. You can then work to bring about compromises that you favor—understanding, of course, that you will sometimes succeed in these efforts and will sometimes fail. Win a few; lose a few. In this situation, you may see the wisdom and fairness of complying with some laws you disagree with on the assumption that others will comply with laws that *you* like and they don't. And if the system is federalist in nature (as it is under the American Constitution) you may have some ability to select a jurisdiction to live in that is relatively more favorable to your views, interests, and principles. But if you know that all of the laws reflect a single coherent set of principles that you disagree with, or that you view as wrong and oppressive, your situation comes to look hopeless. When a law disfavors you, it will not be a case of having lost *this time*. Rather, insofar as you disapprove of the governing principles, you can expect to lose *all the time*. Why would you prefer this situation over one in which the law reflects compromises and trade-offs?

Dworkin attempted to defend his "community of principle" account by invoking a value he called "integrity." We respect people who have the "integrity" to be true to their principles, he observed, even if we disagree with those principles. From that observation, he went on to infer that citizens who view the law as the product of a "single, coherent set of principles" will perceive the law as having this sort of integrity, and will thus understand themselves to be obligated by the law even if they reject the principles that inform it. Conversely, citizens who view the law as the product of compromises will not regard it as legitimate[83] (even, it seems, if the citizens favor or approve the compromises).

Probably there is a valid if limited point in these observations. Sometimes we do admire a person who appears to live with integrity, even if we disagree with that person's beliefs or commitments. But the observation holds within a very limited range. We are hardly brought to admire a Hitler or a Stalin—or a sexual predator or child molester—by the observation that the person actually has, say, a predatory philosophy of life and is living consistently in accordance with that philosophy. Even more importantly, there is a vast difference between admiring someone for their integrity and agreeing that they should have some sort of legitimate authority over you. The fact that someone whose principles I believe to be fundamentally wrong lives sincerely and consistently in accordance with those principles may elicit some respect from me and yet intensify my determination *not* to be subjected to the governance of that consistently misguided (in my opinion) person.

In sum, Dworkin was correct to observe that the "consent of the governed" account of law's authority trades on fictions. But his alternative "community of principle" account—which was his justification for insisting that the Constitution must be viewed as a repository of principles—also rests on a blatant fiction. And in terms of the criteria for measuring the viability of such fictions—plausibility and payoff—Dworkin's account fares far worse than the traditional "consent" account.

FRAGMENTING THE REPUBLIC

Even so, it would be a mistake not to acknowledge the satisfaction that may come from believing that we are living under the governance of principles, not just pragmatic compromises. Because there *is* powerful appeal—isn't there?—in the idea of a life (and perhaps, if only it were possible, a community) of principle. Just in the abstract, we do admire a person who lives with integrity in accordance with some set of moral principles. Many of us aspire to do that ourselves. And it would be comforting to suppose that our political community and our legal system were based on a set of just principles.

Indeed, as we saw in the last chapter, many of the Republic's founders desired to have such a government. They went into the Philadelphia convention carrying some such ideal. During the course of the convention they found that the ideal had to be sacrificed in order to construct a document that had some chance of actually being adopted, thus preventing national disintegration. In this respect, however, our own situation might seem to be more fortunate. We have not had to fight a revolutionary war, as they did, and perhaps we don't need to make the sacrifice of principle that the Constitution's framers were required to make.

This last observation might help to explain the seemingly irresistible appeal of a principled Constitution in recent decades to both liberals and conservatives. The explanation might go like this: "Everyone—or nearly everyone—understands that it would be preferable to live under a principled constitution. The founders *wanted* that, but they learned that they couldn't have it, because a principled constitution wouldn't have been adopted. By contrast, our situation is different in this respect, and more fortunate. We already have a Constitution; we don't need to get it adopted. So we are now free to transform that Constitution into the sort of thing that everyone agree would be ideal."

Some such thinking is arguably implicit in the approaches that both modern scholars and modern justices have taken to the Constitution. A principled constitution is a luxury that the founders could not afford, but that we *can* afford. So why not? Take Justice Brennan's formulation. It would be exhilarating and ennobling—wouldn't it?—to live under a constitution that was a "sublime oration on the dignity of man." True, just reading the text of our own Constitution with untinted eyes, we might have to conclude that it isn't even remotely like that kind of thing. Even so, it is possible to treat the Constitution *as if* it were such an oration. We know this is possible because, as with baptism by immersion in the old joke, we've seen it done—by Wechsler and Dworkin and Balkin and Justice Brennan and so, so many others. So why not?

So the appeal of this way of thinking is understandable enough. And yet as the years go by, it becomes increasingly apparent that such thinking reflects a serious miscalculation. It may be true that our Constitution has already been adopted, and indeed has achieved the stability that comes with two-plus centuries of acceptance. Even so, the founders' concern about national disintegration has not thereby been rendered irrelevant. On the contrary, that concern is as urgent today as it has been at any point since the Civil War, and perhaps since the founding era.

So, yes, we have a Constitution in place. And, thankfully, one of the major sources of division in those earlier decades—namely, slavery—is no longer a source of contention (although of course the broader issues of race and racism are still intensely divisive). And yet in another sense the chasms that separate Americans today run even deeper. Lincoln in his magisterial Second Inaugural Address observed that although Americans had disagreed about the specific institution and practice of slavery, they had shared a basic moral framework: both Northerners and Southerners "read the same Bible and prayed to the same God." Today it is at that more fundamental level that Americans disagree.

Thus, in his seminal study of America's culture wars,[84] the sociologist James Davison Hunter found that across a variety of seemingly discrete issues ranging from education to family to media to law and politics, Americans were increasingly coalescing into two broad and contending camps, which he labeled "orthodox" and "progressive."[85] The former group maintained continuity with—while the latter rejected—the old, biblically oriented civil religion.[86] Though living side-by-side as Americans, orthodox and progressive citizens held to moral conceptions so different that each effectively inhabited "a separate and competing moral galaxy."[87]

Hunter's diagnosis was originally greeted with skepticism by some critics. But in the ensuing three decades, the polarization he described has become ever more conspicuous, and severe. One consequence is a proliferating demonization of those who disagree. Thus, the major political parties seem categorically incapable of perceiving their opponents as anything other than vile and mendacious. Unable to work together constructively, they instead adopt Shermanesque "scorched earth" policies on one or another issue—a tax bill, a judicial nomination, an impeachment. Startlingly high percentages of citizens foresee the possibility of civil war.[88] And talk of secession, once confined to a tiny lunatic fringe, has become more familiar—and emanates from both the left and the right.[89]

These developments are complex, of course—the product of any number of different factors and influences—and the relation of such developments to constitutional law and interpretation is also complex. Despite this complexity, however, two observations might be offered with moderate confidence. First, the notion that constitutional law and rights can be formulated by courts and legal scholars on the confident assumption that the nation's essential unity can be taken for granted now seems naive. Second, the transformative developments in constitutional law that have been undertaken under the heading and in the name of of the "principled" Constitution—developments such as the creation of rights to abortion and same-sex marriage—have been one factor contributing to the cultural polarization.

Thus, in a recent book, Columbia law professor Jamal Greene decries the modern ascendency of what he calls the "rightsism"[90] associated with the constitutionalism advocated by jurists like Brennan and scholars like

Dworkin. This approach is, as Greene's subtitle puts it, "tearing America apart." Greene explains:

> Our opponent in the rights conflict becomes not simply a fellow citizen who disagrees with us, but an enemy out to destroy us. . . . With stakes this high, polarization should not just be expected but is indeed the only sensible response. . . . Conflict over rights can encourage us to take aim at our political opponents instead of speaking to them. And we shoot to kill.[91]

Greene thus concludes that "we . . . are hurtling toward tragedy."[92]

This is a sobering judgment, and one that should put us in mind of the challenge faced by the founders. They discovered that they had to choose between a principled Constitution and a diverse but legally and pragmatically unified nation. It was a wrenching choice, but in the end the framers chose unity. We have supposed that we do not face any such gloomy choice. But it increasingly appears that our supposition has been mistaken.

NOTES

1 Bruce A. Ackerman, "Constitutional Politics/Constitutional Law," *Yale Law Journal* 99, no. 3 (1989): 459–60.

2 Justice William J. Brennan, Jr., "To the Text and Teaching Symposium, Georgetown University," speech, October 12, 1985, https://fedsoc.org/commentary/publications/the-great-debate-justice-william-j-brennan-jr-october-12-1985.

3 For elaboration, see Steven D. Smith, *The Constitution and the Pride of Reason* (New York: Oxford University Press, 1998), 73–83.

4 Cf. Charles Taylor, *Sources of the Self* (Cambridge: Harvard University Press, 1989), 306 ("No one really thinks that disengagement entered the culture from the pen of Descartes, or individualism from that of Locke. Obviously these are influential thinkers; but they are just as much articulating something which is already in train as they are helping to define its future direction and form. . . . They are doing both these things. ").

5 Ibid., 307.

6 Herbert Wechsler, "Toward Neutral Principles of Constitutional Law," *Harvard Law Review* 73, no. 1 (1959).

7 See Fred R. Shapiro and Michelle Pearse, "The Most Cited Law Review Articles of All Time," *Michigan Law Review* 110, no. 8 (2012), 1483, 1489.

8 Cf. Richard A. Posner, *Overcoming Law* (Cambridge: Harvard University Press,1995), 74–75 (citations omitted):

> [Wechsler's] article does not fail to mention the famous cases he had argued in the Supreme Court, and it harps on the deep liberal sympathies that make it painful for him to expose the inadequacies of the Supreme Court's racial jurisprudence– but his sense of

craft permits no less. Assisted by its occasion and its setting, the article richly illustrates the "ethical appeal" of classical rhetoric, in which the speaker enhances the persuasive power of his argument by persuading the audience that he is the kind of person who ought to be believed whatever he says.

9 347 U.S. 483 (1954).
10 Wechsler, "Toward Neutral Principles," 12.
11 Ibid., 15.
12 Ibid., 15 (emphasis added).
13 Ibid., 12.
14 Ibid.
15 Ibid.
16 Ibid., 15 (emphasis added).
17 Ibid., 15.
18 For discussion of the difficulties, see Larry Alexander & Ken Kress, "Against Legal Principles," in *Law and Interpretation: Essays in Legal Philosophy*, ed. Andrei Marmor (1995),279.
19 Wechsler, "Toward Neutral Principles," 16–17.
20 Ibid., 16.
21 Ibid., 17.
22 Ibid.
23 Ibid., 17 (quoting Chief Justice Taney).
24 Ibid., 17.
25 Ibid., 16.
26 See, e.g., Anthony D'Amato, "Aspects of Deconstruction: The Failure of the Word 'Bird,'" *Northwestern University Law Review* 84, no. 2 (1990); Anthony D'Amato, "Aspects of Deconstruction: The 'Easy Case' of the Under-Aged President," *Northwestern University Law Review* 84, no. 1(1989).
27 Wechsler, "Toward Neutral Principles," 17–18.
28 Ibid., 18–19.
29 Ibid., 19.
30 Ronald Dworkin, *Law's Empire* (Cambridge: Belknap Press,1986), 109.
31 Ibid., 190.
32 Ibid., 191.
33 Ibid., 192.
34 Ibid., 194.
35 Ibid., 193–95.
36 Ibid., 195–216.
37 Ibid., 214.
38 Ibid., 166.
39 Ibid., 211.
40 Ibid., 225.
41 Ronald Dworkin, *Freedom's Law: The Moral Reading of the American Constitution* (Cambridge: Harvard University Press, 1996), 74.
42 Ibid., 2; see also ibid., 343 ("The great constitutional clauses set out extremely abstract moral principles that must be interpreted before they can be applied, and

any interpretation will commit the interpreter to answers to fundamental questions of political morality and philosophy.").

43 Ibid.
44 Ibid., 7.
45 Ibid., 10.
46 Ibid., 72.
47 Ibid., 72–73.
48 Ibid., 78.
49 Ibid., 110.
50 Ibid., 125.
51 Ibid., 38.
52 See, e.g., Jack M. Balkin, *Constitutional Redemption: Political Faith in an Unjust World* (Cambridge: Harvard University Press, 2011), 1–8, 33–72; Jack M. Balkin, *Living Originalism* (Cambridge: Belknap Press, 2011), 64–69.
53 Balkin, *Redemption*, 228 (emphasis added).
54 Balkin, *Living Originalism*, 14.
55 Ibid., 14, 25, 23.
56 Ibid, 59.
57 Balkin, *Redemption*, 11.
58 E.g., Balkin, *Living Originalism*, 3, 23, 39–40, 43.
59 Ibid., 3.
60 Ibid., 17; Balkin, *Redemption*, 5–6.
61 E.g., ibid., 6.
62 Ibid., 18–23.
63 See, e.g., Dworkin, *Law's Empire*, 407.
64 Balkin, *Living Originalism*, 69–73.
65 Larry D. Kramer, *The People Themselves: Popular Constitutionalism and Judicial Review* (New York: Oxford University Press, 2005).
66 See, e.g., John Hart Ely, *Democracy and Distrust* (Cambridge: Harvard University Press, 1980); Michael J. Perry, *The Constitution, the Courts, and Human Rights* (New Haven: Yale University Press, 1982).
67 See Jack M. Balkin, "Original Meaning and Constitutional Redemption," *Constitutional Commentary* 24, no 2 (2007): 451; Jack M. Balkin, "Abortion and Original Meaning," *Constitutional Commentary* 24, no 2 (2007): 304.
68 Balkin, "Original Meaning," 494, 501.
69 347 U.S. 483 (1954).
70 See, e.g., Earl M. Maltz, "Originalism and the Desegregation Decisions– A Response to Professor McConnell," *Constitutional Commentary* 13, no. 3 (1996).
71 See Robert H. Bork, *The Tempting of America* (New York: Free Press, 1990), 82.
72 See, e.g., Katz v. United States, 389 U.S. 347 (1967).
73 For discussion, see Steven D. Smith, "That Old-Time Originalism," in *The Challenge of Originalism*, ed. Grant Huscroft & Bradley W. Miller (New York: Cambridge University Press, 2011), 228.
74 Alexander Meiklejohn, *Political Freedom* (New York: Harper, 1960), 9.

75 Rogers Smith, *Liberalism and American Constitutional Law* (Cambridge: Harvard University Press, 1990), 4 (emphasis added).

76 Ronald Dworkin, *Law's Empire*, 194.

77 See Steven D. Smith, *Fictions, Lies, and the Authority of Law* (Notre Dame: University of Notre Dame Press, 2021), 20–23.

78 For elaboration, see generally Smith, *Fictions*.

79 See Akhil Reed Amar, *America's Constitution: A Biography* (New York: Random House, 2005), 5–18.

80 Ronald Dworkin, *Law's Empire*, 211.

81 Ibid., 225.

82 See Bruce Ackerman, *We the People: Transformations* (Cambridge: Harvard University Press, 1998), 110–16.

83 Ronald Dworkin, *Law's Empire*, 178–84.

84 James Davison Hunter, *Culture Wars: The Struggle to Define America* (New York: Basic Books, 1991).

85 Ibid., 43–44.

86 See ibid., 120–25.

87 Ibid., 128.

88 See, e.g., Adam K. Raymond, "How Close is the U.S. to Civil War? About Two-thirds of the Way, Americans Say," *New York Intelligencer*, October 24, 2019, https://nymag.com/intelligencer/2019/10/americans-say-u-s-is-two-thirds-of-the-way-to-civil-war.html

89 See, e.g., Bruce Frohnen, "A Tale of Two Nations," *Chronicles*, July 2021, https://www.chroniclesmagazine.org/a-tale-of-two-americas/; Nathan Newman, "The Case for Blue State Secession," *The Nation*, February 10, 2021, https://www.thenation.com/article/politics/secession-constitution-elections-senate/; F. H. Buckley, *American Secession: The Looming Threat of a National Breakup* (New York: Encounter Books, 2020).

90 Jamal Greene, *How Rights Went Wrong: How Our Obsession with Rights is Tearing America Apart* (New York: Mariner, 2021), 58.

91 Ibid., xvii.

92 Ibid., xxxv.

Chapter Three

So You Think You Want a Constitution of Principles

Larry Alexander

Is a constitution of specific rules, such as two senators for each state, or a requirement presidents must be at least thirty-five years of age, a less attractive constitution than one containing soaring principles or that is itself an expression of a single unifying principle (àa la Dworkin's Integrity[1])? Is the United States Constitution, to the extent it is not a repository of principles and does not exhibit principled integrity, an inferior supreme law as compared to other, more principled constitutions? We have raised doubts of our own about the superiority of more principled constitutions, or more principled readings of them. But the question deserves further investigation.

JUST WHAT ARE "PRINCIPLES"?

As a preliminary matter, we must first determine what principles are and how they differ from such "unprincipled" constitutional rules as two senators per state. Principles are norms—standards of behavior. They thus are members of the same genus as rules and standards. Rules are norms that are relatively determinate and either apply or do not apply. (Dworkin calls them "weightless" norms because of this.[2]) "Drive 55," "come to a complete stop at stop signs," and "two senators per state" are examples of rules. Because they are relatively determinate, they are easy to apply in most cases. They settle what should be done for people who otherwise hold quite divergent moral and political views. How many senators each state should have has been settled by a constitutional rule, even though, as we have seen, there were (and still are) quite divergent views about how many senators each state should have.[3]

Standards are norms whose applications are indeterminate within a certain range. They are typically expressed in language that is vague, with terms such as "reasonable," "substantial," "fair," and "just." For example, "drive at a reasonable speed" expresses a standard.[4] So does a command not to search unless one has "reasonable cause" to do so.[5] And standards, unlike rules, do not settle what is to be done. Only a series of decisions applying the standards—that is, determining what speed is reasonable in certain circumstances, or determining what "reasonable cause" requires—will settle the matters the standards do not settle and gradually "rulify" the standards.[6] And like rules, standards either apply or do not apply.

Principles, however, are different from rules and standards in two ways. First, they cannot be captured by any verbal formulation. It is not that their verbal invocations are vague, though they are. It is rather that no verbal formula can tell one how to apply the principle in any particular circumstance. And that is because of a second differentiating feature of principles, namely, the feature of "weight." Principles incline one's conduct in a certain direction, but they can be outweighed by competing principles.[7]

So principles are norms with weight. Unlike rules and standards, which either apply or do not apply, principles are always potentially applicable, but when applicable may fail to determine a result because of competing principles. We know where rules and standards come from; they are posited by human beings. But where do principles come from? Do they come from morality? Or do they come from the law?

Principles as Moral Norms

Most moral philosophers believe that there are moral principles, principles that ultimately determine which actions are right and which are wrong. And these principles are not the products of human acts. They have not been legislated into existence by humans, nor can humans "repeal" them. They stand outside of human affairs and judge them.

Now it may seem obvious that we would want our Constitution to be a moral one and thus in accord with moral principles. And if that is true, then wouldn't we want provisions in the Constitution that would invalidate any laws that moral principles would condemn?

There are two ways we might incorporate moral principles in a constitution. One way is through a clause, or through an unwritten constitutional norm, to the effect that no law will be deemed valid if it offends moral principles. The second way is through incorporating specific moral principles in the text.

The problem with the first way is that it leads either to anarchy or else to imposing some person's or persons' understanding of moral principles, an understanding that may well be incorrect and will almost surely be controversial. It will lead to anarchy if no person or persons can impose their understanding of moral principles on those whose understanding differs. On the other hand, if some persons' understanding of moral principles—say, the understanding of five Supreme Court justices—*can* be validly imposed on those whose understanding differs, then the supremacy of moral principles will in practice be the supremacy of some specific persons' quite fallible views of moral principles. (Try to imagine the confirmation proceedings for Supreme Court justices if their views of moral principles were regarded as the supreme law of the land. Senator Windbag: "I hear, Ms. Nominee, that you are a fan of John Rawls. But do you think the requirements of public reason should trump religious beliefs?")[8]

One might think that the application of at least some moral principles would not be controversial. Consider Madison's and Wilson's principle of proportional representation, a principle that we will assume is a moral principle for purposes of this point. Isn't proportionality just a matter of ratios? And how can ratios be controversial?

Madison and Wilson assumed the principle of proportional representation just meant allocating representatives according to the states' populations. The more populous the state, the more representatives it should get. And the senate was inconsistent with this principle.

But the populations of states consisted of eligible voters, citizens, aliens, and—until 1863—slaves. Which of these groups should be included in the denominator in order to get the ratios relevant to proportional representation? The Supreme Court in *Evenwel v. Abbott* decided that the total population is the correct answer for equal protection purposes.[9] But whether or not that decision is the correct reading of the Equal Protection Clause, is it the correct understanding of the (putative) moral principle of proportional representation?

Moreover, if proportional representation is a moral principle, it is surely not the only one. And because one moral principle can be outweighed by others, were Madison and Wilson right to assume that their principle of proportional representation was not outweighed by competing moral principles, principles that supported compromising to keep the slave states in the union?

Finally, we've asserted that if laws must be consistent with moral principles, the reality would be that the operative moral principles would be merely some person's or persons' understanding of those moral principles—perhaps the understanding of five Supreme Court justices.[10] But would we even have a Supreme Court? Or Congress? Or a President? Those institutions are created by the rules and standards in the Constitution. But is, say, Congress what true moral principles would prescribe for a legislature? Are its powers consistent with true moral principles? And the same can be asked of all the structural provisions in the Constitution. Are they morally ideal, what true moral principles would prescribe?

What is at stake here is whether, if we are to be governed by correct moral principles, we could even settle on the institutions that would then settle other moral questions. For example, we cannot assume the Supreme Court will be the expositor of governing moral principles unless we actually have a Supreme Court and all the rules about how justices are selected, how long they serve, and so on. And if these rules themselves require settling controversial moral questions, then we will most assuredly end up with no institutional framework for settling anything. The principal reason we have law to guide us rather than Spike Lee's "do the right thing" is because we need to settle many matters that "do the right thing" will not settle. And settlement is itself a moral imperative, even if, as will always be the case, the settlement is morally imperfect.[11]

Let us turn to the other method of incorporating moral principles in the Constitution, that of referring to specific moral principles directly. There are many legal scholars who believe that is what the authors of the Constitution and its amendments have done.[12] For example, they believe that "the freedom of speech" mentioned in the First Amendment is a moral principle. Likewise for "equal protection of the laws."

Ask yourself, however, whether there are such moral principles. If there aren't, then the relevant language in the First and Fourteenth amendments can't be referring to them. I have raised doubts about the existence of a free speech principle, and Peter Westen has famously argued that "equality" is an empty idea.[13] If they are right, then the First and Fourteenth amendments cannot be referring to moral principles, or at least not to principles of "free speech" and "equality."

It is also worth noting that the most popular normative theories of our era—utilitarianism, libertarianism, Rawlsian liberalism, prioritarianism—all have their versions of equality and their own position on speech, but none includes a free speech principle or an equality principle. (Egalitarianism is, of course, equality writ large; but no one believes the Equal Protection Clause mandates thoroughgoing egalitarianism.)

It seems to us very doubtful that any of the terms that appear in our Constitution were intended to refer to principles that actually exist in morality's ontological cupboard, or if they were so intended, that the Constitution's authors succeeded in referring to them.

Principles as Legal Norms

If the case for finding moral principles in our Constitution is weak, what about the alternative—namely, that there are principles in the Constitution, but they are *legal*, not moral, principles? Perhaps our preceding focus on moral principles was wrongheaded, and the principles that we should have been seeking belong to the genus legal, not the genus moral. Is the case for legal principles in our Constitution stronger than the case for moral principles?

We think not. Although moral principles almost surely exist, even if incorporating them in the Constitution is probably not a good idea, the existence of legal principles is altogether another matter. For it is difficult to see how legal principles *could* exist.

Let us examine the views of three exponents of legal principles. Perhaps the most notable of these is Ronald Dworkin. For Dworkin, legal principles, which have the attributes of all principles—non-algorithmic formulations and weight—are principles that both fit the legal rules, standards, and decisions and make them as morally attractive as possible.[14] The dimension of fit applies not only synchronically—no "checkerboard statutes"[15]—but also diachronically. That is, legal principles are to make the past record of coercive government actions as morally attractive as possible.[16] So even if many of the laws and decisions that are products of past governmental acts are morally regrettable or surely morally suboptimal, legal principles show those acts to have the virtue of integrity.[17] In other words, they were the product of a "principled" government and thereby justified the government's coercive acts.

There are several problems with Dworkin's account of legal principles. For one thing, it is impossible to derive the weight of a principle from the laws and decisions it purports to justify, no matter how numerous these laws and decisions.[18] Just to illustrate the problem, let us take Dworkin's perhaps favorite legal principle, "no man may profit by his own wrong."[19] That principle, says Dworkin, was responsible for the court's decision in *Riggs v. Palmer*,[20] which disallowed a murderer from inheriting from his victim despite the relatively clear black letter rule in his favor. Of course, people do profit from their wrongs in several other ways: they take others' real property through adverse possession; they steal others' property but get to keep it when the criminal and civil statutes of limitations have run; they breach contracts and still profit after remedying the breach;[21] and so on. So what is the weight of the principle "no man should profit from his wrong"? If the legislature shortens the statutes of limitation for adverse possession and for theft, does it violate the principle? Change it? We think that because there is no "there" there, these questions are on a par with "are unicorns white or are they beige?"

Even more serious, it is difficult to see the attractiveness of adhering to past incorrect and unjust decisions—that is, the attractiveness of integrity so described.[22] "Sure, I committed some wrongful acts in the past, but now I feel I have to continue committing them. It's a matter of integrity, being principled."

Of course, Dworkin does say that "fit" need not be total, that one can treat some past decisions as "mistakes" and ignore them.[23] But one can't ignore too many, even if they were morally mistaken, because that would make fit superfluous and turn legal principles into moral principles.

Even checkerboard compromises, which give each principled side of a policy issue less than their principles demand, can be justifiable. Dworkin objects to them as unprincipled, which they surely are from one vantage point. But if one thinks social peace and stability are morally worthy goals, then from another vantage point they can be quite principled. Dworkin's legal principles not only justify the unjustifiable but also fail to justify the justifiable.

Another proponent of distinctly legal principles is the German jurisprudent Robert Alexy. His notion of a principle is the same as Dworkin's—a norm that lacks a canonical formulation and has the dimension of weight.[24] And it is quite clear that Alexy's legal principles are not moral principles. For example, he believes there can be a legal principle of "maintenance and support of the manual arts," which is surely not a moral principle.[25] Indeed, Alexy even believes there can be a morally obnoxious legal "principle" of racial segregation.[26]

So how does Alexy believe such legal principles come to exist? He does not agree with Dworkin that legal principles are the most morally attractive principles that fit (to an unspecified degree) with the extant legal rules and decisions. Rather, Alexy believes legal principles can be enacted and in this respect are just like legal rules and standards.[27]

The problem, however, is that it is just flat-out impossible to enact weight. One can enact rather complex rules that state the various conditions in which they apply and do not apply. But such rules will still be, in Dworkin's terms, "weightless." That is, they will either apply or not. And if they do apply, they will determine the result. Principles are not supposed to be like that. So enacting a principle with weight differs from enacting a complex rule. And the difference is that while the latter is possible, the former is not. (We invite the reader to consider for herself how she would specify a norm's weight.)

The final proponent of a "principled constitution" is Mitchell Berman.[28] Berman's notion of a principle is the same as Dworkin's and Alexy's. Like theirs, his principles are legal principles, not moral principles. And according to Berman, the U.S. Constitution, or at least U.S. constitutional law, is replete with legal (constitutional) principles.

Unlike some constitutional scholars—Jack Balkin is an example[29]—Berman does not claim that his constitutional principles are found in particular textual clauses and phrases. Indeed, Berman's focus is less on textual exegesis and more on what he describes as the practice of constitutional law. And in that practice one will find the invocation of various legal principles, such as "federalism," "majority rule," and "precedent."[30] These principles have weight, though their weight varies with the circumstances of the case at hand.

And where does Berman believe these principles and their weights come from, given that they are not enacted in the constitutional text? His answer is that they are derived from the beliefs of those engaged in the practice of constitutional law—presumably lawyers and judges.

But how exactly is that supposed to work? Take three people whose beliefs Berman would say determine the existence and nature of constitutional principles—Alfred, Betty, and Carla. And suppose the question is what is the scope and weight of the constitutional principle of federalism in a case involving, say, a question regarding the extent of Congress's legislative powers. Alfred believes federalism as a principle has broad scope and great weight, so he thinks Congress is intruding too much into areas rightfully left to the states to control. Betty, on the other hand, believes federalism has broad scope but little weight, so she believes Congress is acting within its power. And Carla believes there is no such thing as a federalism principle and so thinks the issue in the case at hand must be resolved solely based on the best interpretation of the text. If that is at all a realistic portrayal of what those engaged in the practice of constitutional law might believe about federalism, how does one determine the principle's scope and weight?[31]

Moreover, there is something odd about a "believing it so, makes it so" theory of constitutional norms. If the beliefs of legal actors are the primal pools from which constitutional principle emerge, what exactly is the content of those beliefs? Does Alfred believe the principle of federalism has the scope and weight it does because *he* believes it? Because he thinks others believe it?[32]

We think Berman's account of the ontology of legal principles is completely untenable, just as are Dworkin's and Alexy's. If we are searching for principles in our Constitution or constitutional law, they cannot be *legal* principles. And we have argued why putting moral principles in the Constitution, while perhaps theoretically possible, would be quite undesirable—indeed, ironically, *morally* undesirable. The most plausible reading of the U.S. Constitution is that it is not a repository of principles, and it's a good thing it is not.

So if legal principles, as such, do not exist, and the only principles we can possibly have are moral principles, would it be desirable if our Constitution contained them (or was "read" to contain them)? We have already given reasons for why that would not be desirable. Governmental officials, be they legislators, presidents, administrators, or judges, already know that they should act in accord with moral principles, at least to the extent the law permits. (What they should do when the law conflicts with what they perceive moral principles require is, of course, a much-mooted and fraught matter, one that we shall elide here.[33])

So officials know that they must act in accord with moral principles when the law otherwise permits. Would the situation be improved if the law required them so to act? That is, if however clear the law otherwise was, they would understand that moral principles were higher law and should be followed?

We have already indicated why we doubt that incorporating moral principles in the Constitution might be, not a good idea, but a very bad one. But let us recapitulate. If the constitutional text purported to pick out specific moral principles, there is no assurance that there would be actual moral principles that corresponded to the ordinary meanings of those provisions. Moreover, even if the Constitution did not do this, but instead incorporated "moral principles" as such, the Constitution itself could not settle matters that need to be settled if there was—as there surely would be—disagreement over what true moral principles require. So some institution would have to declare authoritatively what moral principles require of us. And what organ of government would be up to that task? Who would audition for the role of philosopher kings? If that's what a constitution of moral principles entails, to that prospect we say, "No thank you."

NOTES

1. Ronald Dworkin, *Law's Empire* (Cambridge: Belknap Press, 1986), 164–66.
2. Ronald Dworkin, *Taking Rights Seriously* (Cambridge: Harvard University Press, 1977), 26–27.
3. See, e.g., Sanford Levinson, *Our Undemocratic Constitution* (New York: Oxford University Press, 2006) 49–62.
4. This is the basic law in California. *See, e.g.,* Cal. Veh. Code §22350.
5. See, e.g., U.S. Const., amend. IV.
6. See Frederick Schauer, "The Tyranny of Choice and the Rulification of Standards," *Journal of Contemporary Legal Issues* 14, no. 2 (2005), 803.
7. Dworkin, *Taking Rights Seriously,* 25–28.
8. See John Rawls, *Political Liberalism* (New York: Columbia University Press, 1993).
9. 578 U.S. (2016).
10. See Larry Alexander and Frederick Schauer, "Law's Limited Domain Confronts Morality's Universal Empire," *William & Mary Law Review* 48, no. 1579 (2007), 1595–96
11. See generally Larry Alexander and Emily Sherwin, *The Rule of Rules: Rules, Principles, and the Dilemnas of Law* (Durham, NC: Duke University Press, 2001).

12. See, e.g., Ronald Dworkin, "Comment," in A. Scalia, *A Matter of Interpretation: Federal Courts and the Law* (Princeton: Princeton University Press, 1997) 115, 117.

13. See Larry Alexander, *Is There a Right of Freedom of Expression?* (New York: Cambridge University Press, 2005); Peter Westen, "The Empty Idea of Equality," *Harvard Law Review* 95, no. 3 (1982).

14. See Dworkin, *Taking Rights Seriously*, 340–41, 360.

15. See Dworkin, *Law's Empire*, 178–84.

16. See Dworkin, *Taking Rights Seriously*, 340–41, 360.

17. See Dworkin, *Law's Empire*, 164–66.

18. The reason for this is elaborated at some length in Larry Alexander and Kenneth Kress, "Against Legal Principles," in *Law and Interpretation,* ed. Andrei Marmor (New York: Oxford University Press, 1995) 279, 301–04.

19. See Dworkin, *Taking Rights Seriously*, 22.

20. 115 N.Y. 506, 22 N.E. 188 (1889).

21. Consider a case in which a star vocalist agrees to give a concert in a small city and then receives a much more remunerative offer to perform on the same date in Los Angeles. If she breaches the contract, she may still be able to pay damages and end up with more money than had she honored the contract; nor will a court order specify performance of such a contract.

22. SeeAlexander and Kress, "Against Legal Principles," 308–26.

23. See Dworkin, *Taking Rights Seriously*, 304–41, 360.

24. See Robert Alexy, *A Theory of Constitutional Rights* (New York: Oxford University Press, 2002) 45–47.

25. Ibid., 81.

26. Ibid., 61.

27. See Robert Alexy, "Comments and Responses," in *Institutionalized Reason: The Jurisprudence of Robert Alexy*, ed. Matthias Klatt (New York: Oxford University Press, 2012) 319, 329.

28. See Mitchell Berman, "Our Principled Constitution," *University of Pennsylvania Law Review* 166, no. 6 (2018).

29. See Jack Balkin, *Living Originalism* (Cambridge: Harvard University Press, 2011).

30. See Berman, "Our Principled Constitution," 1383–92.

31. See Larry Alexander, "Appreciation and Responses," in *Moral Puzzles and Legal Perplexities: Essays on the Influence of Larry Alexander* (New York: Cambridge University Press, 2018), 407, 433.

32. Ibid.

33. See Alexander and Sherwin, *The Rule of Rules,* 53–95.

Chapter Four

Mushy Constitutional Principles Enabling Puffed-Up Judicial Policymaking

I'm Against, on Principle

James Allan

The other chapters in this book take varyingly skeptical views of the idea or notion that a constitution should be understood—indeed celebrated—as a document that deals in soaring and morally charged principles. Maimon Schwarzschild ponders the role and nature of principles. He shows some modicum of sympathy for their reign in the constitutional architecture of America, while simultaneously noting that being suspicious of principles is itself a principle and that Americans today are starkly divided over principles in the sense of which are right and which are wrong.[1] Larry Alexander considers the big theoretical picture and the problems involved in incorporating principles into a constitution. Steven Smith takes on two tasks. First off, he considers the actual history of the US Constitution, arguing that only the abandonment of principle permitted its actual coming into existence and its ratification. In other words, the desire for unity trumped all else, which was a sort of guiding principle just not one of the soaring, lofty variants that are these days read into it. And that quest of trying to read such amorphous, lofty principles into the constitutional text is Smith's second topic. It is one in which he turns to look at three prominent US constitutional scholars who, despite the actual history, have embraced the notion that the Constitution is more persuasively seen as a repository of these soaring principles than as a dry legal document (one with the tone and text of an insurance policy, if you want a disparaging characterization).

This chapter will be no exception to that generally skeptical tone when it comes to the desirability of bringing together constitutions and principles. In fact, in some ways this chapter of mine will ratchet up the skepticism by arguing that if you are going to have a constitution then it should be Australia-like, one without mushy principles sprinkled throughout it. Or, perhaps better still, we should go for New Zealand-like constitutional arrangements and hence for a setup that shuns written constitutionalism entirely, so that all the delivering of society's principles is done by elected legislators rather than by unelected judges sifting through the entrails of mushy principles, with no more obvious external constraints on them than those on the augurs of old. That, in essence, is what I will argue in this chapter. And, to lay my non-American cards on the table, I do so as a native-born Canadian who has spent his working life in law schools in pre-handover Hong Kong, London, New Zealand and for the last decade and a half in Australia (with a few US, Canadian and British law school sabbaticals thrown in). "Who better to make that sort of argument?," you might think.

Accordingly, in this chapter I will be making my case on both the "ought" and the "is"—the prescriptive and the descriptive—planes. On the "ought" plane my position comes in two parts. Firstly, if we are going to have a written constitution then it should deal in rules (usually the more rigid the better) that leave comparatively little room for judicial policymaking; rather than shun, it should welcome being drafted with the tone and text of an insurance policy; it should be a recipe book that aims to lock things in, not some repository of lofty and soaring principles that are in practice so amorphous that they abdicate outcomes to those in the future, at the point of application, who will then consult their own moral and political druthers; "the drier it is the better" should be the motto; in brief, mushy principles should overwhelmingly be banished from our ideal constitution. Secondly, I will make the ancillary prescriptive argument that written constitutions are not all that they are cracked up to be anyway. It is possible to do without one at all and still do very well. And the reason they are not what they are cracked up to be has much to do with the fact that many, if not most, written constitutions are replete with precisely those mushy principles (or, in today's world, will be taken by those at the point of application to be replete with such principles) that facilitate judicial policymaking—principles that in effect hand debatable and often extremely contentious social policymaking over to the top judges.

On the "is" plane I will consider two common law, English-speaking jurisdictions that as a matter of descriptive fact have exactly those constitutional characteristics—one has a written constitution with a dry, insurance policy, recipe book type tone that deals in rules, not in mushy principles, and the other is the world's preeminent unwritten constitutional setup. I refer, respectively, to Australia and New Zealand.

Now it was tempting for me to start on the normative "ought" plane, to set out my arguments both for keeping amorphous, lofty principles out of the constitutional text of any written constitution as well as for thinking that unwritten constitutionalism (that leaves all decisions about how to give legal life to mushy principles to the elected legislators) is pretty attractive. Do that and then turn to look at my two real-life jurisdictions, that was my first impulse. Yet on reflection I opted to resist that temptation and to write my chapter the other way round—first give the readers a brief overview of two jurisdictions that have in fact gone down my preferred paths and then, second, make the "ought" argument for why they got it right.

FIRST TWO JURISDICTIONS THAT SHUNNED PUTTING MUSHY PRINCIPLES INTO A WRITTEN CONSTITUTION

Australia—Madison Mark I

Let us start with my home of the last sixteen years, Australia. I have no clear idea how many Americans (or even American constitutional law scholars) know this fact, but Australia probably has the world's most American written constitution. The Australian founders in the late nineteenth century looked around for what they could copy and opted to mimic the United States rather than Canada. Australia's Constitution is more or less the pre-Bill of Rights Madisonian US Constitution. It is Madison's Mark I version, albeit stuffed into the inherited British Westminster parliamentary model. To give readers just a taste of how American the Australian Constitution is, notice that it copied and mimicked a US-style elected Upper House Senate rather than the Canadian or UK options which were both—and incredibly in the year 2022 both still remain—wholly unelected.[2] That may not strike Americans as odd, but across the democratic world there are really only Australia and Italy with Upper Houses anywhere near as powerful as America's, and Italy has been trying unsuccessfully to change that for a while. Australia also copied the general rule that requires the same number of senators from each state, notwithstanding the disparity of the populations of those states that would be sending those same number of senators to the national capital.[3] The only difference here is that Australia locked in just "the equal number rule" but did not specify any particular locked-in number, leaving it to the elected Parliament to vary how many that might be as time goes by. Not too long ago it was ten senators per Australian state but today it is twelve. Australia also opted to copy the American "one-list" model of federalism rather than the Canadian "two-list" model.[4] It left the choosing of the top state court judges to the states, as in the United States, not to the center, as in Canada. The Australians even mimicked the United States in opting to create a national capital city not part of any state (and whose residents did not have a vote for the Senate or the House of Representatives until the 1970s).[5]

So in big-picture terms Australia virtually flat-out copied American-style bicameralism (very rare in the democratic world) and the American version of federalism. These were (and still are) all delivered by means of dry rule-like constitutional provisions wholly lacking in any soaring or lofty or mushy principles. It is more recipe book than John Rawls or Ronald Dworkin. Yes, all heads of powers provisions are inherently vague at the periphery, thereby requiring discretionary calls at the point of application in federalism disputes. But in such cases the judge's discretion or input is not induced by trying to flesh out or live up to soaring, lofty principles. Put differently, federalism strong judicial review is very different from rights-related strong judicial review.[6]

That said, the Australian founders did not pirate everything they saw in the US Constitution. After much debate in various constitutional conventions, and with a thorough understanding of the then US First Amendment jurisprudence, the Australian constitution-makers comprehensively rejected a bill of rights of any sort. They chose to leave all matters related to free speech and the like (matters often closely linked to the "repository of soaring principles" understanding of what a constitution should be) to the elected Parliament. Indeed, throughout the Australian Constitution there are repeated references to "until the Parliament otherwise provides."[7] There is no plausible way to characterize this as a desire to embody fundamental principles within the Australian Constitution; it was, in fact, precisely the opposite desire at work.

The other main bit of constitutional architecture where the Australians looked to the United States but found its model unappealing was the amending clause or the amending procedures. Australia shunned both the US and Canadian alternatives they then observed, choosing instead effectively to copy Switzerland. The Australian founders and ratifiers went for a direct democracy approach that did not make the political class the ultimate decision-makers as to whether the Constitution could be amended. So where both the American and post-1982 Canadian constitutions make successful constitutional amendment wholly dependent upon winning a specified fraction of the federal and state/provincial legislatures, in Australia the political class does not get to make the 'will we or won't we amend' final call. In essence, s.128 of the Australian Constitution (which sets out the rule governing how to achieve a successful amendment) ultimately allows either jouse of the federal parliament to initiate a constitutional amendment referendum on a simple majority of that house vote.[8] Within two to six months after such passage there must be held a constitutional referendum. To pass, the amendment proposal must receive 50 percent plus one person of those who voted across the country as a whole (leg one), while also winning 50 percent plus one person in more than half the states (leg two, the federalism requirement). I have long argued that in procedural terms this—"you need to get the approval of just over half of your fellow citizens, plus over half of them in a majority of the states"—is a much easier threshold to overcome than what you see in the United States and Canada.[9] Many of my fellow Australian constitutional scholars disagree. That is because of the forty-four proposed amendments that have gone to the voters since Australia came into being, only eight have succeeded. Thirty-six have failed. Yet relying on that fact is to elide or confusethe difficulty of the procedural test that has been laid down and what the substantive outcome or record has been. Yes, over 80 percent of constitutional referenda in Australia have failed (though I note that of the thirty-six failures all but five failed on leg one—they could not win the support of half the Australian voters on the day).[10] But it does not follow from that fact that the laid-down procedural test imposes a comparatively high hurdle to overcome. These thirty-six failed constitutional referenda could just as easily be explained as indicating that Australians on the whole like their constitution and do not want to change it much. In fact, when I look at the results of all forty-four of Australia's constitutional referenda over the past century and more, I find that I overwhelmingly agree with the decisions these referenda produced. Now I suspect that most of my fellow Australian constitutional law professors do not. It does not follow from that, however, that Australia's constitution can be said to impose a procedurally tough amendment hurdle. I say again that in my view it does not. It does, though, remove the political and lawyerly castes from having the sole say.

I mention the amending formula here because it bears on Australia's original decision to forswear an entrenched bill of rights (the absence of which in the constitution makes it much harder, plausibly, to make claims about the document being a repository of lofty, soaring principles rather than a dry legal document). You see from Australia's federation or founding in 1901 there have been two later attempts to amend the constitution specifically to insert some version or other of a bill of rights. Both failed, and failed badly. The latter of those attempts was in 1988. This 1988 amendment proposal to entrench a modest bill of rights lost in every single State of Australia, and obviously in the country as a whole. That actuality goes some extensive way to shutting off any claims along the lines of "well, Australians might have wanted the dry, recipe-like constitution back in 1901 but today they want a soaring, lofty, infused-with-principles model." True, that may well be what the vast preponderance of the country's professoriate in the law schools want, as well as what the rest of the lawyerly caste wants—namely, a sort of "repository of lofty principles" model. As a matter of fact, it seems pretty clear to me that that is exactly what both do want. Yet regardless of that, and because Australia's amending formula forces the voting public to be consulted before any constitutional change can occur, we can confidently assert that the evidence is clear that the wider Australian public is happy with a constitution that has the tone and text of an insurance policy.[11] This Australian constitution looks much like your Madison Mark I constitution that delivers the checks and balances you find with strong bicameralism and federalism, albeit where they have been crammed into the Westminster parliamentary model. What is next to nowhere on display in the Australian constitution are soaring principles. Still, by any comparative standards whatsoever Australia's constitution has been a success. Surprising as it may be to some, Australia's constitution is one of the democratic world's oldest continuously in-operation constitutions. I can only think of the constitutions of the United States, Switzerland, and Canada (in that order) as older than Australia's, though there may be one or two others. The point is that dry, recipe-book-type constitutions can work, stand the test of time, and be widely supported by those who live under them. We know this for a fact because that is the case with Australia.

New Zealand—No Principle Other than the Principle of Non-Justiciability

Take a moment to try to number the democracies in the world that can—even at a stretch—be considered to have unwritten constitutions. There is New Zealand. Until the recent Brexit vote in the United Kingdom that took several years to come to fruition[12] New Zealand was without doubt the preeminent parliamentary sovereignty, unwritten constitutional setup in the world. With Brexit decided, and the UK slowly serpentining its way out of the European Union (with that supranational organization's overarching written constitution, disguised as a treaty, having applied to Britain while it was a member state), Britain now rejoins this unwritten constitution club of mine as the preeminent jurisdiction with parliamentary sovereignty at its heart. And lastly, at a stretch, we might be able to include Israel—a country that has some basic laws and an extremely activist top court interpreting them, so that putting Israel into this unwritten camp is very debatable. But it is just plausible. And that is that.

Here, I am going to use New Zealand just because of all the complications surrounding the United Kingdom's attempts to disentangle itself from the EU. Anyway, New Zealand inherited its unwritten constitutional model directly and solely from the UK so most all of what I will say about New Zealand also applies (or soon will) to the post-Brexit UK.[13] I will be brief in this section as I have written about New Zealand and its parliamentary sovereignty constitutional arrangements elsewhere.[14] Let me here just give readers enough of an outline of the New Zealand constitutional arrangements to afford me support for my upcoming prescriptive argument that written constitutions are not all that they are cracked up to be anyway; that it is possible to do without one at all and still do very well; and that the reason for that is largely because New Zealand-style unwritten arrangements do not inject mushy principles into an overarching written constitutional text and thereby facilitate judicial policy making at the point of application of that written document. More bluntly, New Zealand does not hand debatable and often extremely contentious social policy making over to the top judges.

At the heart of a democracy without a written constitution is parliamentary sovereignty—the notion that the elected legislature is legally unlimited, though not morally or politically unlimited. There is judicial review of administrative actions in a parliamentary sovereignty jurisdiction but no strong judicial review, no review by judges of *any* enacted legislation whereby those judges—in the name of mushy principles or of anything else—are empowered to invalidate or strike down legislation. So turn back to New Zealand. Are there limits on power there? Of course there are. Can those limits largely or overwhelmingly be traced back to one over-arching document, as in Canada, Australia, and the United States? No. Limits on power in New Zealand flow from a bunch of statutes, all of which can be altered in the normal way by parliament. And they flow from conventions, and more there perhaps than elsewhere. Most obviously they flow from elections and the democratic process. Yes, it is an incredibly democratic setup, each generation being left to vote for Members of Parliament ("MPs") who, through parliament, can do what they think is best (motivated by whatever wider principles they find most compelling). Hence more than a few Canadians or Americans might wonder, "But where are the legal limits on what the elected parliament can do?" And the answer is, the limits on parliament are not legal. They are moral and political. New Zealanders vote for MPs who more or less share their moral worldview. And if shared morality is too ephemeral for your likings as a power constraint, well, the limits put on MPs by the desire to get reelected are powerful limits indeed. Democracy is a potent check on the scope of action of the lawmaking legislature.

Now some readers may well balk at this point, still thinking that what is needed is to have legal and constitutionalized limits on what the elected legislature can do. For such readers, notice that all those legal limits have to be overseen by real-life people. So in the United States they are overseen by its Supreme Court, by nine judges. And if you live in the United States (or Canada, or South Africa, or Germany, etc) what sort of limits are there that control what those nine ex-lawyers can do, that ensures their interpretations are honest and not the fulfilment of their own unconstrained druthers? Well, there are moral limits, the attachment felt by such top judges to applying the law as written and so in accordance with their oaths of office—as opposed to just making things up at the point of application because some outcome or other seems morally superior to them, or preferable on other grounds. Oh, and there are political limits, as in the extent to which they can withstand criticism in the press when they go wayward. But let us say—and this is hypothetically speaking you understand—but let us say that you think that in some recent case a majority of those top judges (say five out of nine because all top courts happen to be brutally majoritarian institutions, five votes always beating four no matter the quality of the reasoning) just made something up. They pretended to be interpreting the United States Constitution when supposedly "discovering" some implied but nowhere enumerated fundamental new right that these top judges then used to invalidate some law that had been on the statute books for ages. In other words, pick a case where you think the judges lied or made it up—perhaps in the service of mushy principles, perhaps even in the service of mushy principles that you yourself find compellingly attractive. Are there any legal or constitutional limits on those top judges, other than political and moral limits? Of course not. In any setup you will end up having some group of real-life human beings whose actions are constrained, or not constrained, solely by morality and politics. So pick your poison. In New Zealand, with its unwritten parliamentary sovereignty constitution, it is the legislature that lacks legal limits.

Or, if we translate that idea into the language of principles, there are no principles infused into (or reposed in) the New Zealand constitution other than the principle of the non-justiciability of statutes. Sure, all sorts of laws enacted by the legislature in New Zealand were no doubt motivated by principles of varying degrees of mushiness.[15] But none could be challenged in the courts. None was justiciable under a strong judicial review regime of the sort that is virtually taken for granted in my native Canada and in the United States.

AND NOW THE OUGHT CASE AGAINST MUSHY JUSTICIABLE PRINCIPLES

I have sketched out two jurisdictions that share a common law inheritance with the United States. Australia has a written constitution that was the result of unashamedly copying the American constitution, but the first Madisonian version without the Bill of Rights. As we saw, it overwhelmingly deals in rigid rules that leave very little room for judicial policymaking; it is drafted with the tone and text of an insurance policy or recipe book that aims to lock in federalism and bicameralism, not to be the repository of lofty and soaring principles. Meanwhile New Zealand has no written constitution at all.

It is the democratic world's archetypal parliamentary sovereignty jurisdiction. There is no written constitution there that is replete with mushy principles because there is no written constitution at all. Any dealing in principles is the preserve of the legislators, not of the judges.

Having done that I shift now to the "ought" question. And a first point to make is that the desire of those at the point of application—the judges—to be able to make social policy under the guise of giving life to soaring, lofty principles runs high and is powerfully felt by them. I have set out above Australia's recipe-book-like constitution and the failed attempts to inject a bill of rights into it, the last such attempt being in 1988. What I should say here is that in 1992 the High Court of Australia "discovered" (in the "text and structure" of a written constitution that nowhere mentions this and that no actual human beings back at the time plausibly intended) that there existed an implied freedom of political communication principle, one that presumably had lain dormant for over nine decades.[16] This principle-driven and rights-related striking down of legislative power is nowhere mentioned in the Australian constitution. Nor did any of the drafters or framers or ratifiers of the Australian constitution—the people treated as having had the legitimate authority to impose this constitution on Australia's citizens—intend a committee of seven unelected ex-lawyers to have this immense power. You cannot point to real-life people back then who explicitly intended this outcome, nor who believed it was so obvious that judges would have the power that it need not be stated explicitly. Indeed, the evidence is clear and patent that the drafters debated such a First Amendment Bill of Rights-type power being given to the judiciary and they explicitly rejected that option. Instead, nearly a century later, there was a judicial "discovery" that this power had been implied into the overall text and structure of the Australian constitution—with this "discovery" taking place only four years after a failed attempted constitutional referendum to put this power explicitly into the constitution, an attempt in which some of the judges were involved on the "let's put it in" side.

This 1992 "discovered" implied freedom was over time entrenched by the judges, with each successive case's judicial gloss (and variously articulated restrictive permutations) being piled on to earlier glosses and with ever less frequent passing references to the original *ACTV* five-step reasoning: reasoning that starts with the constitution's section 7 reference to "directly chosen by the people" (as regards how the senate must be elected), and mushrooms out from that phrase to an end point that supposedly justifies handing a striking down power for breaching a vague "freedom of political communication" principle to a committee of unelected ex-lawyers. Yes, it is only in certain rather circumscribed circumstances that this implied freedom has been held (by the judges) to afford (to these same unelected judges) the power to decide whether the purpose of a law is legitimate, whether a law is reasonably appropriate and adapted to advance a legitimate object, whether it places a burden on the freedom and if so whether such burdens can be justified, whether other less-restrictive measures are available, whether the law is necessary, and so on and so forth. Yes, between that 1992 case and today there have only been five other times when the High Court of Australia has actually decided to invalidate a statutory provision. So it is by no means widely used. But that is because the basis for doing so—the grounds the judges claim give them this power—is so unbelievably implausible and patently illegitimate. Without any actual bill of rights and with such a clear constitutional history rejecting any such abdication of these sort of calls to the judges, the use of this "implied freedom" power is constrained. It is too obviously self-serving for judges to use in all but a handful of cases. At least that is the case if, like me, you believe that this whole, entire "implied freedom" edifice in Australia rests on the most implausible, unconvincing reasoning imaginable—that the emperor has no clothes and that any impartial outside observer would agree with that sentiment.[17]

So I mention that judicial innovation not because it plays much of a role in Australian constitutional life. It does not. I mention it to show the powerful appeal, to judges, of a system where lofty, soaring principles can be called in aid to strike down statutes passed by the democratically elected legislature.

I turn now to the main "ought" question, to why I think the constitutional arrangements of Australia and New Zealand are better options than Canadian-style or US-style written constitutions that are taken by those at the point of application to be replete with mushy principles. And the gist of my case is that those mushy principles facilitate wide-ranging judicial policymaking; they serve to hand debatable and often extremely contentious social policymaking over to the top judges. As my coauthor Larry Alexander has noted in his chapter, the supremacy of moral principles in any human institution is, in practice, the supremacy of some specific persons' fallible moral views. That is true always and everywhere. In the context of a written constitution taken to be replete with principles it will be the fallible views of the top judges (or rather of those of them who happen to be in the majority in any particular case) that will dictate how these amorphous principles play out in particular circumstances. It will be a handful of ex-lawyer judges who take these principles from their homes up in the Olympian heights of moral abstraction and give them actual effect down in the quagmire of day-to-day decision-making as regards issues over which reasonable, nice people disagree and often disagree strongly. That, in short, is the problem—that this model of written constitutionalism laden with mushy principles gives far too much social policymaking power to an unelected judiciary. It significantly undercuts democratic decision-making.

Take the issue of same-sex marriage. In New Zealand, Australia, Britain, Ireland and many other democracies the choice was made democratically—or as that can be a loaded term, with much argument over whether democracy is best understood in morally Spartan or morally pregnant terms,[18] let us just say that in those places the decision was made either by the elected representatives of the people accountable for their decisions at the next election (Britain, New Zealand) or after a binding referendum on the issue via direct rather than representative democracy (Australia, Ireland). Those options seem to me to be far more legitimate ways to make this decision, and ones that will leave behind them far fewer lingering resentments, than a procedure whereby the country's top nine judges appeal to mushy principles, then vote among themselves, then resolve the issue of same-sex marriage for 320 million Americans[19] or 35 million Canadians.[20] Those "do it through the legislature or by referendum" options also leave open the possibility that a future coalition of voters, should they become a majority, could overturn this call. That is the compromise or bargain at the heart of democratic decision making. When, instead, issues are resolved by proclaiming what lofty, soaring principles supposedly demand—by telling us all what our near-transcendent rights now are (5–4 judicial vote notwithstanding)—it is considerably harder for those on the losing side to respond. Or to reconcile themselves to the fact they lost. Or so it seems to me. Just look at the abortion debate in the United States, where the judges alone made the final call, and compare how it still festers and weeps there whereas near on anywhere else in the democratic world it does not.

Or let us remind ourselves, in a rough-and-ready sort of way, of the sorts of issues on which committees of ex-lawyers have the final say when deciding cases in which mushy principles have been reposed or infused into the country's written constitution.

They, the judges, decide whether democratically mandated restrictions on abortion can stand.[21] They decide the same as far as euthanasia goes.[22] As we just saw they decide whether there will be same-sex marriages. They overturn immigration laws by insisting that each and every refugee claimant must be given an oral hearing (at huge taxpayer expense and with security implications).[23] They overturn democratic legislation aimed at restricting private health care and bolstering a public-only, socialized health care regime.[24] They strike down capital punishment laws.[25] They rewrite criminal procedure laws to favor the accused to a much greater extent and against the judgment of the electorate and their representatives.[26] And, of course, they decide the balance to be struck between health and safety concerns (including restricting tobacco advertising) and free speech (including by tobacco companies),[27] whether incarcerated prisoners must in all cases be allowed to vote,[28] and even whether limits on the salaries of provincially appointed judges in the context of a civil service-wide freeze can stand.[29]

And that is just an off-the-cuff sampling of the sorts of issues and decision-making powers that are given to judges when mushy principles are taken to have been infused into a written constitution. It is the fallible moral and political views of a small handful of ex-lawyer judges (rather than of the tens of millions of voters) that are brought to bear to make the final call on same-sex marriage, socialized medicine, abortion, capital punishment, euthanasia, the whole array of criminal procedures, immigration laws, and a whole lot more. The mushy, amorphous principles are not self-applying after all. Nor is how they should be applied somehow morally self-evident, so that all right-thinking people would make the same exact calls. No, when principles are reposed into the written constitution the effect is to take all sorts of social policy decisions away from the voters and give them to the lawyerly caste from which top judges are chosen. That seems to this non-American to be a very undesirable constitutional arrangement. It is more government for the people (according to us top judges, as modern-day auguries) than it is by the people.

Nor, as we have seen, is it in any way the only option on the table. A written constitution of rigid rules works at least as well.[30] Australia's effectively embodies a commitment to parliamentary sovereignty within the confines of federalism. That being the case, my view when it comes to written constitutions is that "the drier it is, the better" should be our motto. Mushy principles should overwhelmingly be banished from our ideal constitution. Written constitutions that are replete with mushy principles (or, that have been taken by those at the point of application to be replete with such principles) allow far too much room for judicial policymaking. They hand far too many last-word calls over debatable and often extremely contentious social policy debates to the judicial class. They take us too near juristocracy. So I am highly skeptical of the desirability of bringing together constitutions and principles.

NOTES

1. For a similar view see Gary Lawson, "What is 'United' about the United States?" *Boston University Law Review* 101, no. 5 (2021). Lawson makes this point in unequivocal, and at times humorous, terms.

2. The Upper House in the United Kingdom is the ancient House of Lords, until relatively recently a wholly hereditary body but today much more an "appointed for life" body with a smallish cohort remaining of the hereditary sort of peers. Canada's Upper House, known as its senate, is comprised wholly of appointed members. They are appointed by the prime minister with no gainsaying or second-guessing by anyone other than, possibly, the prime minister's cabinet colleagues. As a result of being wholly unelected both these upper houses, in today's democratic world, have little

(for some zero) legitimacy. Hence they rarely, if ever, block any legislation passed by the lower house—to do so would amount to the patently undemocratic body blocking the will of the democratic body. The formal limits on Britain's House of Lords began with the Parliament Act 1911 which limited the unelected House of Lords' power to delay Money Bills to only one month and non-Money Bills to two years (assuming passage by the House of Commons in three successive sessions). Then the Parliament Act 1949 reduced the latter of those delaying powers in the hands of the unelected House of Lords down to one year (assuming passage by the House of Commons in two successive sessions). For my discussion of a leading British constitutional case that centered on the Parliament Acts of 1911 and 1949, see James Allan, "The Paradox of Sovereignty: Jackson and the Hunt for a New Rule of Recognition?" *King's Law Journal* 18, no. 1 (2007). One thing Australia got to first, right off the bat and before America, is that its senate was specified as having to be "directly chosen by the people of the State," and this call was made when the US Senate was still indirectly elected.

3. In the United States, California is the largest state with about 40 million people and Wyoming is the smallest, with about 580,000 people. That makes one's vote for the US Senate worth about 69 times more in Wyoming than in California. In Australia the most populous state is New South Wales with some 8 million people. The least populous is Tasmania with about 550,000. That makes the senate vote of a Tasmanian worth about 14.5 times that of a New South Welshman.

4. A historical irony is that Australia did this, like the United States, aiming to have relatively strong component States. Canada went down the two-list road so as to circumscribe the power of the constituent provinces—they would only get what was in their list, anything not found in either list going to the Feds. This was because Canada federated two years after the US Civil War with a huge Union Army just across the border and memories in Canada strong of the War of 1812 which was initiated by President Madison and the United States (meaning that for Canadians Madison is rightly seen as a legislative genius but not as much of a president, though we Canadians do feel that we won in 1812 given that it was a draw and we did not start it). Here, though, is the irony. Canada aimed for a highly centralized form of federation and yet today has very powerful provinces. In the United States and Australia the respective top courts have, over time, enervated the power of the states—by a modest amount in the United States and by an absolutely huge amount in Australia, to the point that some think it is federalism in name only. For a full account of this emasculation by the courts of Australian federalism, see James Allan and Nicholas Aroney, "An Uncommon Court: How the High Court of Australia has undermined Australian Federalism," *Sydney Law Review* 30, no. 2 (2008): 245.

5. It was a federal compact model, in other words, where those living in territories or districts (as in Washington, DC, or Canberra's Australian Capital Territory or Australia's Northern Territories) did not get to vote for the senate or house. That lasted in Australia until 1975 and the top court's decision in *Western Australia v Commonwealth (First Territory Senators' Case)* [1975] HCA 46. The Commonwealth government (i.e., the Feds) there won against the states in a 4–3 top court decision and

parliament was able to legislate so that Australia's two territories elect two senators each, as compared to twelve from each state.

6. Or so I have argued at length. See James Allan, "Not in for a Pound—In for a Penny? Must a Majoritarian Democrat Treat All Constitutional Judicial Review as Equally Egregious?" *King's Law Journal* 21, no. 2 (2010).

7. For just a sample, see sections 7, 10, 22, 29, 30, 31, 39, 46, 47, 65, 67 and more of the Australian constitution.

8. If you are wondering to yourself "how do the states initiate the amendment machinery?" the answer is "they cannot." This is a clear flaw that has made it impossible for them to combat an *uber*-centralizing top court. Of course at the time of federation, just before the rise of party politics in its virulent form of today, the founders and ratifiers assumed that the senate—the states' house—would look after the interests of the states. That is a laughable thought today.

9. See, for example, note 4 above. Note that in the United States constitutional amendments need a two-thirds vote of both houses of Congress plus approval from three-quarters of the state legislatures. In Canada, for most things, you need a majority of both houses of parliament in Ottawa and then that of two-thirds of the provincial legislatures so long as they represent over half the Canadian population—but for some key matters (such as whether to end the constitutional monarchy) you need *all* the provincial legislatures to agree, even Prince Edward Island's, a province with a population of 160,000 people in a country, Canada, with 38 million. In my view, this latter one lays down what is in practical terms an impossible test to meet.

10. And that is virtually all of the eligible voting population as Australia has, and since 1924 has had, compulsory voting. So there is no scope to argue something along the lines of "only 50 percent of voters voted in this constitutional amendment referendum and so the fact the 'No' vote received 60 percent of the ballots cast means that only 30 percent of the voting population actively signaled their desire to reject the change." I do not mean that I am persuaded by such arguments. I mean that they simply cannot be made in the Australian compulsory voting context.

11. To buttress this claim, I would note that after the 1988 failed referendum advocates of a national Australian bill of rights gave up on the entrenched, constitutionalized model and turned toward pushing for a British or New Zealand-style statutory model. Again, all those efforts have so far failed at the national level. See James Allan, "You Don't Always Get What You Pay For: No Bill of Rights for Australia," *New Zealand Universities Law Review* 24 (2010) and James Allan, 'Why Australia Does Not Have, and Does Not Need, A National Bill of Rights," *Giornale di Storia Constituzionale* 24, no 2 (2012).

12. I discuss that battle for Britain to leave the European Union, one I favored, in James Allan, "Democracy, Liberalism and Brexit," *Cardozo Law Review* 39, no. 3 (2018).

13. And of course likewise to the pre-1972 UK before it joined the precursor organization that became the European Union.

14. See, for example, James Allan, "Informal Constitutionalism and the Role of Politics," *E Publica Direito E Politica* 5, no. 3 (2018); James Allan, "Against Written Constitutionalism" *Otago Law Review* 14, no. 1 (2015); and, in a book that has just

come out titled *The Age of Foolishness: A Doubter's Guide to Constitutionalism in a Modern Democracy* (Academica Press, 2022). What I say here more or less tracks what I say about New Zealand in those pieces.

15. After all, New Zealand was the first country in the world to grant women the franchise; it gave the native Maori men the vote way back in 1867 (even reserving a set number of seats for them); it was one of the first countries to enact social welfare legislation; it wholly rejigged its flailing *dirigiste* economy in the 1980s toward a free-market, free-rade outlook (to the extent its farmers today receive the world's lowest subsidies, almost none, and it has never lost a WTO case to any other country). All these ground-breaking laws were, one assumes, motivated by the lawmakers' attachment to principles. Some might at times have described them as mushy principles. Yet none of these legislative decisions of the New Zealand parliament, or any others, is able to be challenged in the courts on the basis of vague, amorphous, constitutionalized principles that can be invoked by the judges.

16. This happened in the case of *Australian Capital Television Pty Ltd v Commonwealth* [1992] HCA 45. For a discussion of this case and the so-called "implied rights" jurisprudence generally, including by Jeff Goldsworthy, Adrienne Stone, Nicholas Aroney, Katharine Gelber, Ian Callinan, Tom Campbell and others, see the 2011, vol. 30, no. 1, special edition of the *University of Queensland Law Journal* dedicated wholly to this topic.

17. See, for example, James Allan, "Constitutional Interpretation Wholly Unmoored from Constitutional Text: Can the HCA Fix Its Own Mess?" *Federal Law Review* 48, no. 1 (2020).

18. I argue for the morally thin or procedural understanding as preferable in James Allan, "Thin Beats Fat Yet Again—Conceptions of Democracy," *Law & Philosophy* 25, no. 5 (2006).

19. *Obergefell v Hodges*, 576 US ___ (2015).

20. *Halpern v Canada (AG)* [2003] OJ 2268 (Ont CA).

21. *Roe v Wade*, 410 US 113 (1973); *R v Morgentaler* [1988] 1 SCR 30.

22. *Washington v Glucksberg*, 117 S Ct 2258 (1997); *Carter v Canada (A-G)* [2015] 1 SCR 30.

23. *Singh v Canada (Minister for Employment and Immigration)* [1985] 1 SCR 177.

24. *Chaoulli v Quebec (Attorney General)* 2005 SCC 35.

25. *Roper v Simmons*, 125 S Ct 1183 (2005).

26. In Canada, *R v Askov* (1990) 74 DLR (4th) 355, then an extrajudicial rationalization and apology for that decision in the 26 July 1991 edition of *Lawyers Weekly* (vol 11, no. 13) followed by the recanting of *Askov* in *R v Morin* (1992) 72 CCC (3d) 11 (SCC). In the United States, *Miranda v Arizona*, 384 US 436 (1966).

27. *RJR MacDonald Inc v Canada* (1995) 127 DLR (4th) 1, a dozen years later modified or recanted in *Canada (Attorney General) v JTI-MacDonald Corp* 2007 SCC 30. And notice that the interpretation of the same right (not just one to free speech, but to others too) leads to varying, indeed sometimes mutually inconsistent, outcomes in differing jurisdictions. See James Allan and Grant Huscroft, "Constitutional Rights Coming Home to Roost? Rights Internationalism in American Courts," *San Diego Law Review* 43, no 1 (2006).

28. *Sauve v Canada (Attorney General)* [1993] 2 SCR 438 and, after lengthy legislative hearings and attempts to soften or ameliorate the ban, *Sauve v Canada (Chief Electoral Officer)* [2002] 3 SCR 519. In the latter of those cases, the chief justice (writing for the 5–4 majority) referred obliquely to countries mentioned in the dissent that disagree with her court's narrow 5–4 ruling as "self-proclaimed democracies" [41], those countries including Australia, the UK, the United States, and New Zealand. Extrapolating from mushy principles seems able to instil a sort of hubris in some top judges.

29. *Reference Re Remuneration of Provincial Court Judges* [1997] 3 SCR 3. Jeffrey Goldsworthy described this case as one of the most blatant instances of judicial self-serving he had ever seen, not to mention the most implausibly reasoned.

30. And even for those like me, who complain that all the recent responses across the democratic world to the COVID-19 pandemic amounted to the worst inroads on our civil liberties in two or three centuries (see, for example, James Allan, "The Corona Virus: Old vs Young," *Griffith Journal of Law & Human Dignity* 8, no. 2 [2020]), it is not as though countries with entrenched bills of rights and written constitutions infused with mushy principles had judges stand up to these overly despotic laws more than they did in Australia and New Zealand. Canada's and the United States' judicial responses to these sort of laws look to have been—and to continue to be—nearly identical to the antipodean judicial responses.

Chapter Five

The Power—and Peril— of Principle

Maimon Schwarzschild

> These are my principles! If you don't like them . . . I have others.
>
> —Groucho Marx

If constitutional and statutory interpretation, and the work of the courts more broadly, ought to draw on political and moral ideals or principles—or by nature cannot fail to do so—if only translucently, and mediated through legal practices and institutions, the question remains how much force the light of principle should exert on the law. The question is all the more difficult because many principles at stake—such as liberty, equality, stability, good government, self-government—are open to conflicting interpretations, and almost regardless of interpretation are sometimes in tension or even in conflict with one another.

It is actually a dilemma that recurs in many areas of life and thought. It is echoed, for example, in the debates in philosophical ethics between deontology—roughly, do justice (whatever you mean by that) and let the heavens fall (if necessary)—and consequentialism, i.e., do whatever has the best consequences (whatever you mean by that) regardless of principle. The slipperiness of the idea of principle is accentuated by the fact that both deontology and consequentialism can be considered principles, as indeed the idea that one shouldn't be principled, or too principled, or too directly principled, is itself a principle.

In American political thought, the dilemma about principle emerges perhaps most acutely among conservative or right-of-center thinkers, although it surely surfaces under various guises in other streams of thought as well.

In the conservative intellectual sphere, there is a sharp division about how devoted to principle politics and adjudication ought to be. Very broadly, there is the view associated with the philosopher Leo Strauss, and especially with some of his students and followers, but also with some constitutional scholars outside the Straussian orbit, that the Constitution gives legal effect to principles laid down in the Declaration of Independence, principles which themselves reflect natural law, and that constitutional adjudication is only true to the Constitution when it is guided by these principles. Against this, there is the view associated with Burke and Michael Oakeshott and their American followers that is suspicious of abstraction and rationalism in politics and law, and hence suspicious of abstract principle, emphasizing instead the importance of tradition, established ways of life, and compromise, especially as against the likely tyranny of utopian theory.

The leading—and most intellectually pugnacious—advocate of the Straussian stance toward principle was the American political philosopher Harry Jaffa. Jaffa insisted that the Constitution embodied principles of civil equality before the law and liberty under law: principles which the courts are obliged to vindicate through active judicial review, especially in constitutional cases. Jaffa was particularly scathing of conservative advocates of judicial restraint, like Robert Bork, who would withdraw, in Jaffa's view, from faithfully enforcing the Constitution's principles.

Jaffa is probably most noted for his studies of Lincoln and for his tireless advocacy for the natural law principles that in Jaffa's view underlay the Declaration of Independence, and hence (in his view) the Constitution. Jaffa argued that these principles were given new life and new force in the words and actions of Abraham Lincoln. Jaffa's study of the Lincoln-Douglas debates, *Crisis of the House Divided*, published in 1959, launched Jaffa's decades-long intellectual campaign. Jaffa had been a student of Leo Strauss at the University of Chicago, and is identified with an intellectual group known as West Coast Straussians. (There is a politically less conservative group of scholars known as East Coast Straussians.) Late in life, Jaffa published a book of his essays on Strauss, including exchanges with critics of Jaffa's anti-relativist and natural-law interpretation of Strauss: Jaffa, not otherwise much of a joker, entitled the book *The Crisis of the Strauss Divided*—pretty funny, actually.[1]

Jaffa, like his teacher Leo Strauss, was an erudite and subtle scholar. Jaffa's and Strauss's insistence on principle was tempered by their commitment to the Aristotelian idea of prudence, practical wisdom, or "phronesis." As Strauss put it, "There is a universally valid hierarchy of ends, but there are no universally valid rules of action."[2] This is no simpleminded or extremist idea of how principle should guide politics and law: far more sophisticated than "let the heavens fall." Yet the essence of Jaffa's position is that the

Constitution adopts and enacts natural law principles, principles given new depth and meaning and authority by Abraham Lincoln, and that constitutional interpretation—and legal adjudication generally—must be guided by these principles.

The followers of Leo Strauss are by no means the only ones on the intellectual center-right who insist that American law and politics should be guided strongly by principle. Richard Epstein and Randy Barnett, for example, take essentially that position, Epstein in particular with the idea that Locke's principles underlie the Constitution, Barnett with the idea that the Constitution and its interpretation, to be legitimate, must be consistent with the principles of the Declaration of Independence. These principles, says Barnett, guarantee the natural rights of each individual person to life, liberty, and the pursuit of happiness: natural rights which are unalienable and hence that no American government has the authority to alter or abolish; rights inherent to We the People, to "each and every one."[3]

The alternative conservative view, suspicious of abstract principle, reflects Burke's and Michael Oakeshott's thought, and tends to associate the politics—and the jurisprudence—of principle with the utopianism of the political left, with its susceptibility to fanaticism and tyranny. Thus Burke rejects the Jacobin principle of the Rights of Man as abstract, extreme, and lacking in practical wisdom, and contrasts it with the "*real* rights of men" derived from tradition, manners, and historically accumulated experience.[4] Along similar lines, Oakeshott criticizes "rationalism" in politics: the idea that there are correct answers in politics, rather than uncertain judgments based on practice and experience.[5] Oakeshott identifies seventeenth-century puritanism, eighteenth-century enlightened despotism, and twentieth-century fascism and communism as examples of principled or ideologically based government. Oakeshott sets what he calls the "enterprise" element of government against the "civil" element: "enterprise" implying a single collective principle or goal or a small number of goals, "civil" implying institutions within whose framework citizens are free to pursue their own diverse and self-chosen goals.[6] Any actual state might have "enterprise" and "civil" elements, but the more civil and the less enterprise, the less domination of some people by others and the less the state will be mobilized to impose a collective purpose on everyone. John Kekes takes essentially this view in his *Case for Conservatism*: "There is no reason to suppose that there is such a thing as 'the best' political arrangements, or that, if there were, their creation and implementation would somehow escape the evil propensities of the people in charge." Kekes's conservatism rejects the "pitfalls of the rationalistic aspirations of absolutism" and says that conservatives "thus differ from liberals, socialists, and others in refusing to make an a priori commitment to the overriding importance of any particular condition or small number of conditions among all those necessary for good lives."[7]

The two contrasting views, to be sure, are tendencies, or ideal types. The principled Straussians and non-Straussians temper their commitment to principle by linking it with prudence, practical wisdom, and institutional experience. The Burkeans and skeptics of rationalism-in-politics are not nihilists about principle: their suspicion of abstract principles is itself a kind of principle, and there is an element of principle in their convictions that politics and law should take account of the pluralism of human values, and should be conducted with due respect for settled ways of life. Yet the two views or tendencies have genuinely diverging practical implications. The strong-for-principles party tends to favor vigorous judicial review: that the courts should readily strike down statutory enactments (and executive actions or administrative rules) that violate applicable principles. Jaffa and Epstein and Barnett, for example, are explicit about this. The skeptics about abstract principles tend to favor judicial restraint: that the courts should be reluctant to interfere with the decisions of elected and answerable officials, at least unless—as James Bradley Thayer put it—the constitution would otherwise be violated "beyond a reasonable doubt."[8]

WHICH OF THE TWO VIEWS IS MORE PERSUASIVE? IS THERE A MIDDLE WAY BETWEEN THEM?

A much older controversy, which in some ways at least echoes this one, might cast some light on the question, and perhaps suggest something of an answer.

There was a split in medieval Jewish thought over whether true beliefs or Jewish peoplehood ought to be considered the highest Jewish value. The Spanish-born philosopher and physician Maimonides (born c. 1135 CE, died 1204) held that rational perfection—above all, true knowledge about God—is the highest value: that only a person who achieves intellectual perfection in this sense fully merits God's providence, might achieve prophecy, and enjoys immortality or "a share in the world to come." The Spanish-born poet, philosopher, and physician Judah Halevi (born c. 1075 CE, died 1141) held, by contrast, that the People of Israel have a unique mystical relationship to God, that they have a kind of divine substance, and that this substance provides the potential to achieve prophecy, which cannot be achieved through human, philosophical reason.

Maimonides wrote in various genres: in Hebrew on Jewish law, in Arabic in his most famous and most difficult philosophical work, his "Guide to the Perplexed." The philosophy of Maimonides was a key topic for Leo Strauss: Strauss's writings about Maimonides may have been his most original and most characteristic. Strauss was notably impressed by the "esoteric" nature of Maimonides's philosophy: namely that Maimonides's most provocative views were often expressed "between the lines," intended only for the most sophisticated readers. (Strauss was surely correct that this was the way Maimonides wrote: Maimonides said so explicitly in the "Guide." Strauss may have been led or misled by his preoccupation with Maimonides to think that many other classical thinkers—if not virtually all of them—were similarly "esoteric" and wrote to hide their true thoughts.) Nonetheless, Maimonides was clear enough that intellectual perfection, full knowledge and acceptance of true principles, is the only path to human flourishing and hence to God's grace.

Maimonides's view has at least two important implications. First, universalism rather than religious or ethnic or racial particularism. Any human being can, in principle, attain divine truth. "Hear the truth from whomever says it," wrote Maimonides, alluding to Aristotle and al-Farabi among Maimonides's non-Jewish intellectual heroes and mentors.[9] Reason, and thus intellectual perfection, is available to anyone: hence divine grace, the gift of prophecy, and "a share in the world to come" are available to gentiles as well as to Jews. The Torah is a good path, perhaps the best path, toward philosophic excellence and divine grace, but implicitly it is not the only one. This was a remarkably generous and open-minded idea in an era when *"extra ecclesiam nulla salus est"*—no salvation outside the church—was so prevalent a doctrine.[10]

The second implication, however, about which Maimonides was explicit, is that there are principles of faith that must be believed: if you are to flourish fully as a human being you must know their truth and be able to prove them. Maimonides famously laid down Thirteen Principles—versified, they are set as a hymn, sung weekly in synagogues to this day—and Maimonides held that anyone who denies or even doubts a single one of these (or at least who denies or doubts one of the first five principles, which are about the nature of God) is a heretic who should be excommunicated and lose all rights as a Jew.

Judah Halevi, by contrast, was a great mediaeval exponent of Jewish particularism, most explicitly in his philosophical dialogue, the *"Kuzari"*—a fictional debate between representatives of Judaism, Christianity, Islam, and Aristotelian philosophy summoned by the King of the Khazars, who in the end is persuaded to convert his kingdom to Judaism.[11] Human philosophy, which suffers from the limits of human reason, is quickly dismissed in the *Kuzari* as a possible path to truth. Instead, God's special providence for the people of Israel establishes the unique essence or divine order of the Jewish people, on a higher level than the rest of creation.

One implication of this is that there can be considerable freedom of thought within the Jewish community. What makes one a Jew is descent from a Jewish mother, not belief in particular propositions or principles. Unlike

Maimonides, Judah Halevi lays down no catechism, from which any dissent (or even doubt) is anathema, heretical, and cause for excommunication. But another implication, explicit in the Kuzari, is a kind of ethnic, racial particularism about the Jewish people.[12] Even converts to Judaism, on this view, cannot really be full Jews. The potential for prophecy—possessed exclusively by the people of Israel—comes from God's special providence, which is conveyed through the generations by Jewish descent. Becoming fully a member of the Jewish people requires many generations of intermarriage with them.[13]

Maimonides's and Judah Halevi's contrasting views are far from simple-minded: both men were complex and sophisticated thinkers, and at least in Maimonides's case, as Leo Strauss emphasized, his real thoughts were often deliberately disguised. Maimonides was genuinely a universalist in his conviction that true principles, and divine grace, are available (in principle) to all. But Maimonides was nonetheless deeply devoted to Jewish law and practice, and to the particular welfare of the Jewish community. As for Judah Halevi, there is the obvious complication that his mystical idea of Jewish heredity was put forward in a book, written in Arabic—not the Hebrew of his poetry—celebrating the conversion of the Khazar kingdom to Judaism.

Yet the two views or tendencies represented, and reinforced, a genuine divergence in Jewish thought and practice. The Maimonidean versus anti-Maimonidean controversy—essentially over the religious validity and importance of reason and scientific philosophy—continued bitterly, complete with book-burnings and "canceling" of opposing views, for centuries after Maimonides's and Judah Halevi's deaths. The tension between the idea of Judaism as a religion of reason with universalist tendencies and Judaism as a more mystical and inward-looking way of life remains to this day, and has been a constant in Jewish history.

In fact, both views have great force from a Jewish point of view. At its best, Jewish life has encompassed both Maimonides's openness to the wisdom of the world—and his welcome to any who wish to share Jewish life—and also Judah Halevi's warm spirit of peoplehood. (At less than its best, Jewish life can yield to dogmatism, seemingly encouraged by Maimonides's Thirteen Principles; and to the ethnic exclusivism implicit, or explicit, in Judah Halevi's writings.) Over the centuries, Judaism has been able to accommodate both the Maimonidean priority for intellectual principle and Judah Halevi's priority for peoplehood, in part because of the "federal" or decentralized character of the Jewish communities. There exists no central Jewish religious authority, no clerical hierarchy. Each Jewish community—ultimately, each individual Jew—chooses its (and his or her) own religious leaders. This makes a kind of pluralism possible, and indeed inevitable.

ARE THERE IMPLICATIONS FOR THE AMERICAN CONTROVERSY, ESPECIALLY ON THE INTELLECTUAL CENTRE-RIGHT, OVER HOW MUCH, AND HOW DIRECTLY, PRINCIPLE SHOULD GUIDE POLITICS AND LAW?

As with Maimonides's and Judah Halevi's contrasting ideas, there is great force both to the Straussian idea that reasoned politics and jurisprudence should be guided by principle, and also to Burkean skepticism of abstract principles. Principle can devolve into fanaticism, or at least into the imposition—judicially or otherwise—of a single principle, or a few related principles, at the expense of conflicting but nonetheless valuable principles. Yet without principle there are few if any standards of right and wrong. (Even the crude principle of vae victis or victory to the strongest is itself a principle.)

There are two American practices or institutions that provide frameworks, and a measure of constraint, for effectuating political principle. One, where adjudication is concerned, is the adjudicative process itself, the body of legal rules and practices which govern the work of the courts. In America, as in other common law countries, constitutional and statutory provisions are interpreted and applied by judges with a common law training and cast of mind, thus in something of a common law style. Common law in turn has a long-standing association with the rule of law, and with certain classically liberal values, among them: respect for the autonomy of the individual; neutrality of legal rules, in the sense that they apply generally, not just to favored or disfavored parties—equality before the law; and legal predictability and fair notice about what the law requires.[14] The common law process allows for development and change, taking political and moral principles into account. Yet there is a difference, in degree if not in kind, between common law-inflected adjudication and the direct administration or imposition of political principles. There is the characteristic common law deference to precedent, without rigid adherence to it. Legal technicality and professionalism impose their own constraints, and there is an ethic—even when it is honored in the breach—of judicial impartiality.

Federalism is a second factor constraining the reign of principle in America. To the extent that state governments have lawmaking jurisdiction, and the national government's powers are limited, there is scope for pluralism and diversity of laws and policies. Some states have higher taxes than others; regulatory burdens vary from state to state; even on a matter of life and death, some states have capital punishment, others do not. State and local laws themselves reflect values and principles, of course, but the principles can vary from state to state, hence diluting the force of any given principle or policy—at least to the extent that a particular principle cannot directly be given nationwide force, by judicial decree or otherwise.

To the extent that these institutions or practices—the adjudicative process, and federalism—constrain the force of principle, or militate against a tyranny of principle, they may create a kind of middle way: between too principled a reign of virtue and too unprincipled a way of law and life. This might appeal, in a general way, to Maimonides, who shared Aristotle's partiality for the via media. It might be at least a tolerable compromise between the Straussian party of principle and the Burkean skeptics about abstract principles or rationalism in politics: presumably with the party of principle continuing to push for more principle—and perhaps for more vigorous judicial review—and the Burkeans pushing the other way.

To what extent this sort of compromise—more or less reflected in America's existing institutions—can continue to accommodate today's conflicting political and moral principles is a more difficult question. Federalism, in the sense of state governments with extensive policy-making authority and a national government with limited power, is itself hard pressed by the reality of an ever-growing and ever-more-powerful federal establishment. The Code of Federal Regulations ran to about 10,000 pages in 1950, 71,000 pages in 1975, 175,000 pages in 2015.[15] The federal government's share of the national economy was approximately 15 percent in 1950, it is about 30 percent today.[16] The number of federal crimes, and the severity of federal sentencing, have grown rapidly in recent decades.[17] In more and more areas of life, Americans live under federal—not state—rules and regulations. Federal rules or policies are essentially uniform throughout the country, and the principles underlying them are not constrained by alternative rules and policies, underlain by alternative principles, in this or that state. Any federal district judge can issue a nationwide injunction, controlling—at least for the time being—the enforceability of a law everywhere in the country.[18] All this opens the way to more or less direct imposition of whatever principle is in the mind or heart of some federal authority, or even of a single federal judge.

Moreover, Americans today—at least many of them—are starkly divided over fundamental principles. Among the contending principles are broadly liberal ones, stressing individual autonomy and freedoms of speech and thought; and principles that are more or less diametrically at odds with these, stressing group rights and reparations, suspicious at best of liberal freedoms. Many Americans, possibly most of them, hold liberal principles to one degree or another; but illiberal or anti-liberal principles have a powerful presence in American colleges and universities, and are increasingly influential in primary and secondary schools, in the media, even in many corporate bureaucracies. Numerous surveys confirm what most of us see, hear, and experience directly: growing mutual antipathy between adherents of conflicting political faiths.¹⁹ With political and ideological allegiance at or near the heart of people's identity or sense of themselves for a growing number of Americans, political principles increasingly take on a quasi-religious cast. All this tends toward irreconcilable enmity between the conflicting political cultures, which sometimes seem to be coalescing into virtually separate political nations.

It can reasonably be replied that American democracy has been bitterly divided at various times in the past: that only once, when the house divided was half slave and half free, has this led to breakdown, secession, and civil war. Mediating institutions and practices, including adjudicative and other legal processes, and a more or less decentralized federalism, have helped to accommodate and to find a modus vivendi among conflicting political and moral principles. Whether these institutions, and Abraham Lincoln's mystic chords of memory and the better angels of our nature, can continue to do so remains to be seen.

NOTES

1. Harry V. Jaffa, *The Crisis of the Strauss Divided* (New York: Rowman & Littlefield, 2012).

2. Leo Strauss, *Natural Right and History* (Chicago: University of Chicago Press, 1953), 162. By contrast, the worldly wisdom of "phronesis" is repudiated as sinful in the thirty-nine Articles of Religion of the Anglican Communion: "the lust of the flesh, called in the Greek φρόνημα σαρκός, which some do expound the wisdom . . . of the flesh . . . hath of itself the nature of sin." Article IX, Articles of Religion, Book of Common Prayer 615 (n.d.).

3. Randy E. Barnett, "The Declaration of Independence and the American Theory of Government: First Come Rights, and Then Comes Government," *Harvard Journal of Law and Public Policy* 42, no. 1 (2019): 23–28.

4. Edmund Burke, *Reflections on the Revolution in France*, ed. John G. A. Pocock (Indianapolis: Hackett Publishing Co, 1987): 51.

5. Michael Oakeshott, *Rationalism in Politics* (London: Methuen, 1962).

6. Michael Oakeshott, *On Human Conduct* (Oxford: Clarendon Press, 1975).

7. John Kekes, *A Case for Conservatism* (Ithaca: Cornell University Press, 1998), 88, 44. Kekes distinguishes "absolutist conservatives" from "skeptical conservatives," absolutists hewing to a narrow body of religious or secular political principles: Kekes stands with the skeptics. "The historical record of societies whose political arrangements were inspired by rationalistic schemes is most alarming," says Kekes. Ibid., 30.

8. *See* James B. Thayer, "The Origin and Scope of the American Doctrine of Constitutional Law," *Harvard Law Review* 7, no. 3 (1893) 129 (arguing that the Supreme Court should only strike down an Act of Congress if it is unconstitutional "beyond a reasonable doubt"). Thayer's actual argument was somewhat narrow: that federal courts should not strike down Acts of Congress unless they are unconstitutional

beyond a reasonable doubt. Thayer supported less deferential review of state laws and executive conduct. Ibid., 154–55. But Thayer has generally been read as putting forward a broader principle of judicial restraint. See generally "One Hundred Years of Judicial Process: The Thayer Centennial Symposium," *Northwestern University Law Review* 88, no. 1 (1993) 1 (a symposium on Thayer's doctrine of judicial restraint).

9. Maimonides, "Eight Chapters" in *Ethical Writings of Maimonides,* Raymond L. Weiss and Charles Butterworth, eds., (New York: New York University Press, 1975), 61.

10. For a scholarly yet very readable introduction to Maimonides's thought, see Menachem Kellner, *Science in the Bet Midrash* (Brighton: Academic Studies Press, 2009). Kellner's essays in this book bear directly on Maimonides' intellectual universalism and intellectual perfectionism.

11. Judah Halevi, *The Kuzari*, trans. Hartwig Hirschfeld (New York: Schocken, 1964). There is controversy among historians over whether the Khazar kingdom—an ethnically Turkic principality in eastern Europe and western Asia—actually was converted to Judaism in or around the eighth century CE, and if so, on what terms and for how long. See Peter B. Golden, "The Conversion of the Khazars to Judaism," in *The World of the Khazars*, ed. Peter B. Golden (Boston: Brill, 2007). But cf. Shaul Stampfer, "Did the Khazars Convert to Judaism?" *Jewish Social Studies* 19, no. 3 (2013) (answering "No").

12. Steven S. Schwarzschild, "Proselytism and Ethnicism in R. Yehudah HaLevi," in *Religionsgespräche im Mittelalter*, ed. B. Lewis and F. Niewoehner (Wiesbaden: Otto Harrasowitz, 1992). In this essay my father z"l seeks some grounds—he concedes that it isn't easy—to mitigate the racial or ethnic doctrines in the *Kuzari*.

13. There are conflicting attitudes toward conversion in the Jewish world to this day. See Marc D. Angel, *Choosing To Be Jewish: The Orthodox Road to Conversion* (Jersey City: Ktav Publishing House, 2005) (welcoming sincere converts to Judaism). But cf. Marc D. Angel, "Thoughts on the Conversion Crisis, Institute for Jewish Ideas and Ideals" (2016) (reviewing the ultra-Orthodox resistance—Rabbi Angel calls it oppression in at least some cases—directed at sincere converts by the Israeli Chief Rabbinate): https://www.jewishideas.org/blog/thoughts-conversion-crisis-rabbi-marc-d-angel

14. See Maimon Schwarzschild, "Keeping It Private," *San Diego Law Review* 44: 677 (2007).

15. See Federal Register, Code of Federal Regulations Total Pages and Volumes 1938–2014: https://www.federalregister.gov/uploads/2015/05/Code-of-Federal-Regulations-Total-Pages-and-Volumes-1938-2014.pdf.

16. C. W. Crews Jr., *Ten Thousand Commandments* (Washington DC: Competitive Enterprise Institute, 2019),26, https://cei.org/sites/default/files/10KC2019.pdf

17. John Baker, "Revisiting the Explosive Growth of Federal Crimes," *The Heritage Foundation,* https://www.heritage.org/report/revisiting-the-explosive-growth-federal-crimes; see also Maimon Schwarzschild, "The Bureaucratic Takeover of Criminal Sentencing," *New Mexico Law Review* 49, no. 1 (2019): 93.

18. See Amanda Frost, "Academic Highlight: The Debate Over Nationwide Injunctions," SCOTUSblog, February 1, 2018, https://www.scotusblog.com/2018/02/academic-highlight-debate-nationwide-injunctions/

19. See, e.g., "The Partisan Divide on Political Values Grows Even Wider," Pew Research Center, October 2017: https://www.pewresearch.org/politics/2017/10/05/the-partisan-divide-on-political-values-grows-even-wider/; see also "In a Politically Polarized Era, Sharp Divides in Both Partisan Coalitions," Pew Research Center, December 2019 ("Partisanship continues to be *the* dividing line in the American public's political attitudes, far surpassing differences by age, race . . . or other factors"), https://www.pewresearch.org/politics/2019/12/17/in-a-politically-polarized-era-sharp-divides-in-both-partisan-coalitions/

Bibliography

Ackerman, Bruce. "Constitutional Politics/Constitutional Law." *Yale Law Journal* 99, no. 3 (December 1989): 453–547.
———. *Foundations*. Vol. 1 of *We the People*. Cambridge: Belknap Press, 1993.
———. *Transformations*. Vol. 2 of *We the People*. Cambridge: Belknap Press, 1998.
Alexander, Larry. "Appreciation and Responses." In *Moral Puzzles and Legal Perplexities: Essays on the Influence of Larry Alexander*, edited by Heidi M. Hurd, 407–40. New York: Cambridge University Press, 2018.
———. *Is There a Right of Freedom of Expression?* New York: Cambridge University Press, 2005.
Alexander, Larry, and Ken Kress. "Against Legal Principles." In *Law and Interpretation: Essays in Legal Philosophy*, edited by Andrei Marmor, 279–327. Oxford: Clarendon Press, 1995.
Alexander, Larry, and Frederick Schauer. "Law's Limited Domain Confronts Morality's Universal Empire." *William & Mary Law Review* 48, no. 5 (April 2007): 1579–1604.
Alexander, Larry, and Emily Sherwin. *The Rule of Rules: Rules, Principles, and the Dilemmas of Law*. Durham, NC: Duke University Press, 2001.
Alexy, Robert. "Comments and Responses." In *Institutionalized Reason: The Jurisprudence of Robert Alexy*, edited by Matthias Klatt, 319–56. New York: Oxford University Press, 2012.
———. *A Theory of Constitutional Rights*. New York: Oxford University Press, 2002.
Allan, James. "Against Written Constitutionalism." *Otago Law Review* 14, no. 1 (2015): 191–204.
———. *The Age of Foolishness: A Doubter's Guide to Constitutionalism in a Modern Democracy*. Washington, D.C.: Academica Press, 2022.
———. "Constitutional Interpretation Wholly Unmoored from Constitutional Text: Can the HCA Fix Its Own Mess?" *Federal Law Review* 48, no. 1 (March 2020): 30–45.
———. "The Coronavirus: Old vs Young." *Griffith Journal of Law & Human Dignity* 8, no. 2 (2021): 198–211.
———. "Democracy, Liberalism and Brexit." *Cardozo Law Review* 39, no. 3 (February 2018): 879–904.

———. "Informal Constitutionalism and the Role of Politics." *e-Pública—Revista Eletrónica de Direito Público* 5, no. 3 (December 2018): 60–75.

———. "Not in for a Pound—In for a Penny? Must a Majoritarian Democrat Treat All Constitutional Judicial Review as Equally Egregious?" *King's Law Journal* 21, no. 2 (July 2010): 233–56.

———. "The Paradox of Sovereignty: Jackson and the Hunt for a New Rule of Recognition?" *King's Law Journal* 18, no. 1 (2007): 1–22.

———. "Thin Beats Fat Yet Again: Conceptions of Democracy," *Law & Philosophy* 25, no. 5 (September 2006): 533–59.

———. "Why Australia Does Not Have, and Does Not Need, A National Bill of Rights." *Giornale di Storia Constituzionale* 24, no. 2 (II Semestre 2012): 35–48.

———. "You Don't Always Get What You Pay For: No Bill of Rights for Australia." *New Zealand Universities Law Review* 24, no. 4 (December 2010): 179–96.

Allan, James, ed. "The Implied Rights Cases: Twenty Years On." Special issue, *University of Queensland Law Journal* 30, no. 1 (2011).

Allan, James, and Nicholas Aroney. "An Uncommon Court: How the High Court of Australia has undermined Australian Federalism." *Sydney Law Review* 30, no. 2 (June 2008): 245–98.

Amar, Akhil Reed. *America's Constitution: A Biography*. New York: Random House, 2005.

Anderson, Benedict. *Imagined Communities*. Rev. ed. London: Verso Books, 2016.

Angel, Marc D. *Choosing To Be Jewish: The Orthodox Road to Conversion*. Jersey City: Ktav Publishing House, 2005.

———. "Thoughts on the Conversion Crisis." *Institute for Jewish Ideas and Ideals*, April 1, 2016, https://www.jewishideas.org/blog/thoughts-conversion-crisis-rabbi-marc-d-angel.

Baker, John. "Revisiting the Explosive Growth of Federal Crimes." The Heritage Foundation, June 16, 2008. https://www.heritage.org/report/revisiting-the-explosive-growth-federal-crimes.

Balkin, Jack M. "Abortion and Original Meaning." *Constitutional Commentary* 24, no 2 (Summer 2007): 291–352.

———. *Constitutional Redemption: Political Faith in an Unjust World*. Cambridge: Harvard University Press, 2011.

———. *Living Originalism*. Cambridge: Belknap Press, 2011.

———. "Original Meaning and Constitutional Redemption." *Constitutional Commentary* 24, no 2 (Summer 2007): 427–532.

Barnett, Randy E. "The Declaration of Independence and the American Theory of Government: First Come Rights, and Then Comes Government." *Harvard Journal of Law and Public Policy* 42, no. 1 (Winter 2019): 23–28.

Berman, Mitchell. "Our Principled Constitution." *University of Pennsylvania Law Review* 166, no. 6 (May 2018): 1325–1413.

Bork, Robert H. *The Tempting of America*. New York: Free Press, 1990.

Buckley, F. H. *American Secession: The Looming Threat of a National Breakup*. New York: Encounter Books, 2020.

Burke, Edmund. *Reflections on the Revolution in France*. Edited by John G. A. Pocock. Indianapolis: Hackett Publishing Co, 1987.

Brennan, Justice William J., Jr. Speech presented to the Text and Teaching Symposium at Georgetown University, Washington, D.C., October 12, 1985. https://fedsoc.org/commentary/publications/the-great-debate-justice-william-j-brennan-jr-october-12-1985.

Crews, Clyde Wayne, Jr. Ten Thousand Commandments: An Annual Snapshot of the Federal Regulatory State. Washington, DC: Competitive Enterprise Institute, 2019. https://cei.org/sites/default/files/10KC2019.pdf.

D'Amato, Anthony. "Aspects of Deconstruction: The 'Easy Case' of the Under-Aged President." *Northwestern University Law Review* 84, no. 1 (1989): 250–56.

———. "Aspects of Deconstruction: The Failure of the Word 'Bird.'" *Northwestern University Law Review* 84, no. 2 (1990): 536–41.

Dworkin, Ronald. "Comment." In *A Matter of Interpretation: Federal Courts and the Law*, by Antonin Scalia, 115–28. Princeton: Princeton University Press, 1997.

———. *Freedom's Law: The Moral Reading of the American Constitution*. Cambridge: Harvard University Press, 1996.

———. *Law's Empire*. Cambridge: Belknap Press, 1986.

———. *Taking Rights Seriously*. Cambridge: Harvard University Press, 1977.

Ellis, Joseph J. *The Quartet: Orchestrating the Second American Revolution, 1783–1789*. New York: Alfred A. Knopf, 2015.

Ely, John Hart. *Democracy and Distrust*. Cambridge: Harvard University Press, 1980.

Frohnen, Bruce. "A Tale of Two Nations." *Chronicles*, July 2021. https://www.chroniclesmagazine.org/a-tale-of-two-americas/.

Frost, Amanda. "Academic Highlight: The Debate Over Nationwide Injunctions." SCOTUSblog, February 1, 2018. https://www.scotusblog.com/2018/02/academic-highlight-debate-nationwide-injunctions/.

Golden, Peter B. "The Conversion of the Khazars to Judaism." In *The World of the Khazars*, edited by Peter B. Golden, 123–62. Boston: Brill, 2007.

Greene, Jamal. *How Rights Went Wrong: How Our Obsession with Rights is Tearing America Apart*. (Boston: Houghton Mifflin Harcourt, 2021).

Guelzo, Allen C. "How Slavery Is and Isn't in the Constitution." *Public Discourse*, November 8, 2018. https://www.thepublicdiscourse.com/2018/11/42658/.

Halevi, Judah. *The Kuzari*. Translated by Hartwig Hirschfeld. New York: Schocken, 1964.

Hunter, James Davison. *Culture Wars: The Struggle to Define America*. New York: Basic Books, 1991.

Jaffa, Harry V. *The Crisis of the Strauss Divided*. New York: Rowman & Littlefield, 2012.

Kekes, John. *A Case for Conservatism*. Ithaca: Cornell University Press, 1998.

Kellner, Menachem. *Science in the Bet Midrash*. Brighton: Academic Studies Press, 2009.

Kramer, Larry D. *The People Themselves: Popular Constitutionalism and Judicial Review*. New York: Oxford University Press, 2005.

Larson, Edward J., and Michael P. Winship. *The Constitutional Convention: A Narrative History from the Notes of James Madison*. New York: Modern Library, 2005.

Lawson, Gary. "What is 'United' about the United States?" *Boston University Law Review* 101, no. 5 (October 2021): 1793–806.

Levinson, Sanford. *Our Undemocratic Constitution*. New York: Oxford University Press, 2006.

Madison, James. *Notes of Debates in the Federal Convention of 1787*. Athens: Ohio University Press, 1966. First published 1840 by Langtree & O'Sullivan (Washington).

Maimonides. "Eight Chapters." In *Ethical Writings of Maimonides*, edited by Raymond L. Weiss and Charles Butterworth, 59–104. New York: New York University Press, 1975.

Maltz, Earl M. "Originalism and the Desegregation Decisions—A Response to Professor McConnell." *Constitutional Commentary* 13, no. 3 (Fall 1996): 223–31.

Meiklejohn, Alexander. *Political Freedom: The Constitutional Powers of the People*. New York: Harper, 1960.

Newman, Nathan. "The Case for Blue State Secession." *The Nation*, February 10, 2021. https://www.thenation.com/article/politics/secession-constitution-elections-senate/.

Oakeshott, Michael. *On Human Conduct*. Oxford: Clarendon Press, 1975.

———. *Rationalism in Politics*. London: Methuen, 1962.

"One Hundred Years of Judicial Process: The Thayer Centennial Symposium." Special issue, *Northwest University Law Review* 88, no. 1 (Fall 1993).

Perry, Michael J. *The Constitution, the Courts, and Human Rights*. New Haven: Yale University Press, 1982.

Pew Research Center. In a Politically Polarized Era, Sharp Divides in Both Partisan Coalitions. December 17, 2019. https://www.pewresearch.org/politics/2019/12/17/in-a-politically-polarized-era-sharp-divides-in-both-partisan-coalitions/.

———. *The Partisan Divide on Political Values Grows Even Wider*. October 5, 2017. https://www.pewresearch.org/politics/2017/10/05/the-partisan-divide-on-political-values-grows-even-wider/.

Posner, Richard A. *Overcoming Law*. Cambridge: Harvard University Press, 1995.

Rawls, John. *Political Liberalism*. New York: Columbia University Press, 1993.

Raymond, Adam K. "How Close is the U.S. to Civil War? About Two-thirds of the Way, Americans Say." *New York Intelligencer*, October 24, 2019. https://nymag.com/intelligencer/2019/10/americans-say-u-s-is-two-thirds-of-the-way-to-civil-war.html.

Rossiter, Clinton, ed. *The Federalist Papers*. New York: Signet Classic, 2003.

Schauer, Frederick. "The Tyranny of Choice and the Rulification of Standards." *Journal of Contemporary Legal Issues* 14, no. 2 (2005): 803–14.

Schwarzschild, Maimon. "The Bureaucratic Takeover of Criminal Sentencing." *New Mexico Law Review* 49, no. 1 (Winter 2019): 93–106.

———. "Keeping It Private." *San Diego Law Review* 44, no. 3 (August/September 2007): 677–94.

Schwarzschild, Steven S. "Proselytism and Ethnicism in R. Yehudah HaLevi." In *Religionsgespräche im Mittelalter*, edited by B. Lewis and F. Niewoehner, 27–42. Wiesbaden: Otto Harrasowitz, 1992.

Shapiro, Fred R., and Michelle Pearse. "The Most Cited Law Review Articles of All Time." *Michigan Law Review* 110, no. 8 (June 2012): 1483–1520.

Smith, Rogers M. *Liberalism and American Constitutional Law*. Cambridge: Harvard University Press, 1990.

Smith, Steven D. *The Constitution and the Pride of Reason*. New York: Oxford University Press, 1998.

———. *Fictions, Lies, and the Authority of Law*. Notre Dame, IN: University of Notre Dame Press, 2021.

———. "That Old-Time Originalism." In *The Challenge of Originalism*, edited by Grant Huscroft and Bradley W. Miller, 223–245. New York: Cambridge University Press, 2011.

Stampfer, Shaul. "Did the Khazars Convert to Judaism?" *Jewish Social Studies* 19, no. 3 (Spring/Summer 2013): 1–72.

Stern, Seth, and Stephen Wermeil. *Justice Brennan: Liberal Champion*. Boston: Houghton Mifflin Harcourt, 2010.

Strauss, Leo. *Natural Right and History*. Chicago: University of Chicago Press, 1953.

Taylor, Charles. *Sources of the Self*. Cambridge: Harvard University Press, 1989.

Thayer, James B. "The Origin and Scope of the American Doctrine of Constitutional Law." *Harvard Law Review* 7, no. 3 (1893): 129–56.

Wechsler, Herbert. "Toward Neutral Principles of Constitutional Law." *Harvard Law Review* 73, no. 1 (November 1959): 1–35.

Westen, Peter. "The Empty Idea of Equality." *Harvard Law Review* 95, no. 3 (January 1982): 537–96.

Index

Ackerman, Bruce, 40, 56
Alexy, Robert, 70
Articles of Confederation, 18
Australia:
    Bill of Rights, lack of, 77–79, 83
    constitution compared to Italian constitution, 77
    and constitutional referenda, 78–79
    implied freedom of political communication, 83–84
    and "Madison Mark I" constitution, 77
    and rule-based constitution, 76
    and speech, freedom of, 78
authority:
    as a political fiction, 55
    and representation, 18

Balkin, Jack, 3, 40, 49–51, 53, 59, 70
Barnett, Randy, 93–94
Berman, Mitchell, 70–71
bicameralism, 77–78
Bork, Robert, 52, 92
Brennan, Justice William, 7–8, 32, 40, 52, 59–60
Brexit, 80
Brown v. Board of Education, 41, 52
Burke, Edmund, 92

Butler, Pierce, 13, 27

causal influences of academic theory, 40
Citizens United v. FEC, 56
Civil War, 27, 30
common law, 97;
    adjudicative process as constraint on force of principle, 98
compromise:
    and judgment by modern constitutionalists, 32–33
    in relation to principles, 15–16, 22–23
    See also The Great Compromise; Three-Fifths Compromise
Congress:
    powers of, 11, 67, 71
    and representation, 15–16
    structure of, 12
Connecticut Compromise. *See* The Great Compromise
consent of the governed, 15, 18–19, 47, 54–58
consequentialism, 91
Constitution:
    as compared with the Declaration of the Rights of Man, 15
    as a legal document, 39–40
    "moral reading" of, 47–49

morality of structural provisions within, 67–68
"original meaning" versus "living constitution," 52–53
Preamble, 15, 30–32
as a "repository of principles," 40, 44
Constitutional Amendment, 78;
Fifth Amendment, 48
First Amendment, 48, 67–68. *See also* speech, freedom of.
Fourteenth Amendment, 30, 46, 48–49, 52, 54, 67
Third Amendment, 49
Fourth Amendment, 52–54
"Reconstruction Amendments," 56
Seventh Amendment, 54
culture wars, 60

Declaration of Independence, 18, 31, 50–51, 54
Declaration of the Rights of Man, 14–15
deontology, 91
Dworkin, Ronald, 3, 40, 47–49, 54–58, 65, 69–70

Ellis, Joseph, 9, 25, 30
Ellsworth, Oliver, 23
Epstein, Richard, 93
Evenwel v. Abbott, 67

federal government, power of, 98
federalism, 78
as constraint on force of principle, 97–98
The Federalist Papers, 10, 18, 25
framers' intent:
and "expected applications," 52–54
and unification of states, 8–9, 33, 39
Franklin, Benjamin, 8, 10, 22
French Constitution. *See* Declaration of the Rights of Man.

French Revolution, 12

Garrison, William Lloyd, 30
Gerry, Elbridge, 23–24
Gladstone, William, 6
The Great Compromise, 16–19, 22–24
Greene, Jamal, 60–61

Halevi, Judah, 95–96
Hamilton, Alexander, 9–10, 12;
and proportional representation, 17–18, 20
Hughes, Charles Evans, Chief Justice, 45
Hunter, James Davison, 60

Jaffa, Harry, 92;
Jefferson, Thomas, 12, 14, 47
judicial policymaking, 81–82

Kekes, John, 93
King, Rufus, 17–18, 23
Kramer, Larry, 51
Kuzari, 95

Lincoln, Abraham, 9, 60
Lincoln-Douglas debates, 92

Madison, James, 9, 18–19, 23–25, 67
Maimonides, 94–96
Marx, Groucho, 91
Martin, Luther, 17
Mason, George, 28–29
Meiklejohn, Alexander, 54
Morris, Gouverneur, 10, 14, 24, 28–29, 31

nationwide injunctions, 98
natural rights, 93
New Jersey Plan, 14
New Zealand:
and democracy, 81
post-Brexit UK, compared with, 80
and unwritten constitution, 76, 81

Oakeshott, Michael, 93
Obergefell v. Hodges, 56

parliamentary sovereignty, 80–82;
    and unwritten constitution, 81
Philadelphia Convention, 6, 16, 27, 59
Pinckney, Charles, 28
Planned Parenthood v. Casey, 56
principles:
    in American politics, 99
    as appealing to judges, 84
    Bill of Rights, relationship to, 79
    Constitution, relation to, 7, 42
    and judicial policymaking, 76, 85
    and legal legitimacy, 54–58
    as legal norms, 68–72
    in mediaeval Jewish
        thought, 94–96
    as moral norms, 44, 66–67
    as "mushy," 75–76, 82, 85, 86
    and natural law, 92
    and philosophical ethics, 91
    as standards of behavior, 65–66
    unification of states, sacrificed
        for, 58–59. *See also*
        compromise

Randolph, Edmund, 9, 24
representation:
    proportionalism, 17–19, 67
    state-egalitarianism, 18–19
Riggs v. Palmer, 69

same-sex marriage, 84–85
Scalia, Justice Antonin, 52
Sherman, Roger, 23, 29–30
slavery, 16;
    compromising on, 27–30, 59–60
Smith, Rogers, 54

speech, freedom of, 68, 78, 98
Strauss, Leo, 92;
    on Maimonides, 94–95
Straussians and non-Straussians,
    compared, 93–94
Strong, Caleb, 24
Supreme Court:
    and judicial reasoning, 42–44
    and "duty of fidelity," 45
    authority of, 15, 26, 41, 67
    New Zealand Members of
        Parliament, compared
        with, 81–82

Taylor, Charles, 40
Thayer, James Bradley, 94
Thirteen Principles of Faith, 95
Three-Fifths Compromise, 29

unification of states:
    challenges of, 11–13
    consequences of disunion, 9–10
universalism, 95

Virginia Plan, 14

Washington, George, 8–9
We the People, 14, 55, 93;
    attempts to define, 19–22
    authority of, 17, 26
    and idealism, 31
    See also consent of the governed
Wechsler, Herbert, 3, 40;
    "Toward Neutral Principles
        of Constitutional Law"
        lecture, 41–47
Westen, Peter, 68
Wilson, James, 17–18, 23–25, 67

About the Authors

Steven D. Smith is a Warren Distinguished Professor of Law at the University of San Diego and co-executive director of the Institute for Law and Religion. He writes in the areas of constitutional law, law and religion, and legal theory. His books addressing constitutional law include *Fictions, Lies, and the Authority of Law* (Notre Dame 2021), *The Rise and Decline of Religious Freedom* (Harvard 2014), and *The Constitution and the Pride of Reason* (Oxford 1998).

Larry Alexander is a Warren Distinguished Professor of Law at the University of San Diego. He is the author or coauthor of seven monographs and the editor or coeditor of five anthologies on jurisprudence, criminal law theory, constitutional theory, and legal reasoning. The publishers include Cambridge University Press (four monographs), Duke University Press, Edward Elgar, and Palgrave. He is also the author or coauthor of 250 published articles, essays, and book chapters on the above topics. He presently teaches Criminal Law and Constitutional Law.

James Allan holds the oldest named chair at the University of Queensland where he is the Garrick Professor of Law. He is a native-born Canadian who practiced law at a large firm in Toronto and then at the Bar in London before moving to teach law in Hong Kong, New Zealand, and then Australia. He has had sabbaticals at the Cornell Law School and the University of San Diego School of Law in the United States, at Osgoode Hall Law School and the Dalhousie Law School in Canada (where he was the Bertha Wilson Visiting Professor of Human Rights), and at King's College Law School in London, England.

Allan has published widely in the areas of constitutional law, legal philosophy, and bill of rights skepticism. His books include *The Age of Foolishness: A Doubter's Guide to Constitutionalism in a Modern Democracy* (Academia Press, 2022), *Democracy in Decline* (McGill Queen's University Press,

2014), and, as coeditor and one contributor, *Keeping Australia Right* (Connor Court, 2020). Allan also writes regularly for weeklies and monthlies, including being a regular contributor to *The Spectator Australia* and *Quadrant* and a sometime contributor to *The Australian, Law & Liberty* and *The Conservative Woman*.

Maimon Schwarzschild is professor of law at the University of San Diego, where he has taught constitutional and international law since 1982. He is an English barrister and an American lawyer: he was an attorney in the Civil Rights Division of the US Department of Justice from 1976 to 1981 and practiced as a barrister in London in the 1980s. He was a visiting professor at the Sorbonne for several years, and has been a visiting professor at the Hebrew University in Jerusalem. He is Director of the Institute of Law and Religion at the University of San Diego and a member of the editorial board of *Law and Philosophy*. He is an associate member of Landmark barristers' chambers in London. He has published extensively on constitutional law, jurisprudence, law and religion, and civil rights. He has recently coedited *A Dubious Expediency: How Race Preferences Damage Higher Education*.

www.ingramcontent.com/pod-product-compliance
Lightning Source LLC
Chambersburg PA
CBHW020128010526
44115CB00008B/1028